Writing Poetry with Children

This resource book provides the information, guidance, and reproducible resources needed to make poetry writing successful and pleasurable for both teachers and students.

Step-by-step lessons make it easy to teach a variety of poetry forms:

- **Couplets**
- **Cinquain**
- **Haiku**
- **Limericks**
- **Shape Poems**
- **Acrostic Poems**
- **Plus a potpourri of additional poetry writing experiences**

Reproducible writing forms on which to showcase students' poetry are provided for more than 30 topics.

Large-print "How to" charts to post help students remember the steps for writing each of the poetry forms taught.

A special section of this book covers lots of interesting ways to display and share student poems.

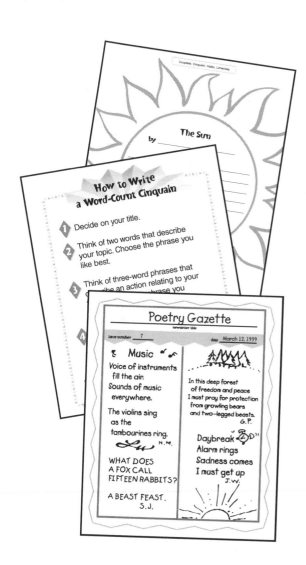

Congratulations on your purchase of some of the finest teaching materials in the world.

For information about other Evan-Moor products, call 1-800-777-4362 or FAX 1-800-777-4332.
Visit our Web site http://www.evan-moor.com. Check the Product Updates link for supplements, additions, and corrections for this book.

Author: Jo Ellen Moore
Editor: Marilyn Evans
Designer: Keli Winters
Illustrator: Cindy Davis and Jo Larsen
Cover: Cheryl Puckett

Evan-Moor
EDUCATIONAL PUBLISHERS
EMC 734

P9-CKA-553

Contents

Resources in
Writing Poetry with Children

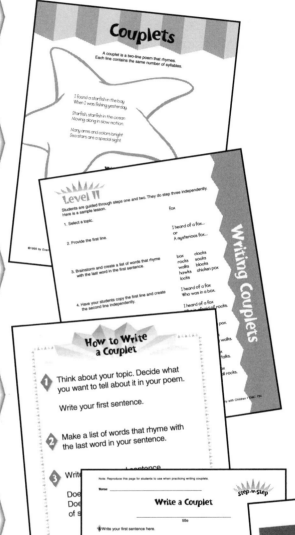

- Samples of each poetry form

- Step-by-step lessons for three difficulty levels

- "How to" charts for each poetry form

- Reproducible "Step-by-Step" forms

- 30 reproducible writing forms

- Ideas for displaying and sharing student poetry

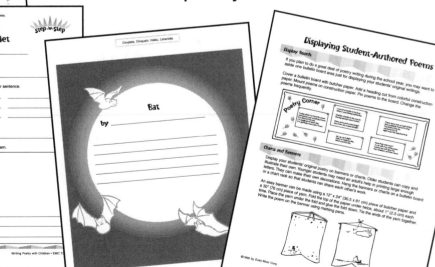

Steps to Teaching Poetry Writing

Plan the Lesson

- Decide which form of poetry you would like your students to learn to write.
  Easier forms: couplet, word-count cinquain, shape poem, acrostic poem
  Harder forms: triplet, quatrain, syllable-count cinquain, haiku, limerick

- Read the introductory page for the poetry form and select samples to share with your students. (Some sample poems are given on each introductory page. Also see the bibliography on page 96 for suggested poetry books.)

- Decide which of the three difficulty levels presented is the most appropriate for your students. Use Level I when you first introduce a poetry form. Progress to the other levels when students are ready.

  Level I—Students are guided through all the steps.
  Level II—Students are guided through the initial steps and complete the poem independently.
  Level III—Students follow the steps independently.

  Optional
  You may wish to make an overhead transparency or a chart of the "How to" writing steps that are provided for each poetry form. Refer to the steps as you proceed through the lesson.

  Reproduce the "step-by-step" form if you want students to write each step as the lesson proceeds.

Prewriting

Before beginning a poetry writing lesson, read the examples of the poetry style that you have chosen. This gives students familiarity with the rhythm and rhyming pattern of that poetry form.

Writing

Follow the steps for the lesson level you have chosen.

Sharing and Publishing

Provide opportunities for students to share their poems with others. This modeling will motivate them to continue writing and be especially helpful for hesitant writers.

Pages 88–94 present ways to display and share original poems.

Couplets

A couplet is a two-line poem that rhymes.
Each line contains the same number of syllables.

I found a starfish in the bay
When I was fishing yesterday.

Starfish, starfish in the ocean
Moving along in slow motion.

Many arms and colors bright
Sea stars are a special sight.

Writing Couplets

- Even very young writers can be successful writing couplets. Do not expect young students to be able to maintain the same syllable count in each line.

- Pages 6–8 present three levels of couplet writing lessons. Use the lesson that seems most appropriate for your students.

- After completing the Level I lesson, you may want students to copy and illustrate the poem.

- Page 11 presents samples of triplets and various forms of quatrains that can be used with older students.

Students are guided through all the steps to write a couplet. Here is a sample lesson.

1. Select a topic of interest to your students.

   cat

   Provide the first sentence. The complexity of the sentence will depend on the level of student writing abilities.

   I saw a black cat...
   or
   Quietly staring, the cat...

2. Brainstorm and create a list of words that rhyme with the last word in the first sentence. (Use a rhyming dictionary or thesaurus with students in grade three or higher.)

hat	fat	sat
pat	mat	vat
bat	rat	flat

3. The class creates the second line of the couplet together. (Ignore syllable count with younger or less able students.)

   I saw a black cat
   Asleep on the mat.

   I saw a black cat
   That was very fat.

   I saw a black cat
   Chasing a rat.

   Quietly staring, the cat
   Was mesmerized by a bat.

   Quietly staring, the cat
   Settled down on her mat.

   Quietly staring, the cat
   Purred as I gave her a pat.

Writing Couplets

Level II

Students are guided through steps one and two. They do step three independently. Here is a sample lesson.

1. Select a topic.

fox

2. Provide the first line.

I heard of a fox...
or
A mysterious fox...

3. Brainstorm and create a list of words that rhyme with the last word in the first sentence.

box	clocks
rocks	socks
walks	blocks
hawks	chicken pox
locks	

4. Have your students copy the first line and create the second line independently.

I heard of a fox
Who was in a box.

I heard of a fox
Who is afraid of rocks.

I heard of a fox
Who had chicken pox.

A mysterious fox
Took long, lonely walks.

A mysterious fox
Howls when he talks.

A mysterious fox
Jumped over tall rocks.

Writing Couplets

Students at this level have had lots of guided practice and are ready to write couplets independently.

- Reproduce the "How to" chart on page 9 on a transparency or post it where students can refer to it while writing.

- Reproduce the step-by-step form on page 10 if students need assistance in the writing process or use any of the topic forms on pages 52–71.

- Students at this level should be guided to revise and rewrite their poems. They might work in pairs or small groups to refine the descriptive vocabulary and adherence to the poetry form. Tell students what you like about their poems *(I think that adjective really paints a picture of your subject.)*, but don't be afraid to offer suggestions for improvement *(Can you think of a two-syllable word to use instead? Then your syllable count will be the same in both lines.).*

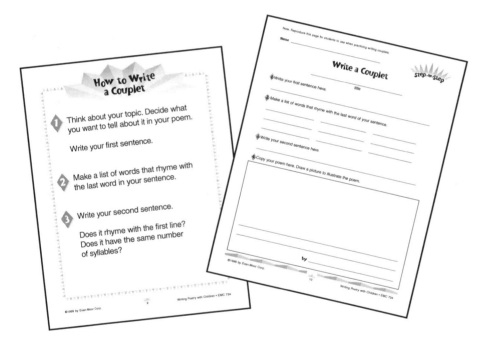

Writing Couplets

How to Write a Couplet

 Think about your topic. Decide what you want to tell about it in your poem.

Write your first sentence.

 Make a list of words that rhyme with the last word in your sentence.

 Write your second sentence.

Does it rhyme with the first line? Does it have the same number of syllables?

Name _____

Write a Couplet

_____
title

1. Write your first sentence here.

_____

2. Make a list of words that rhyme with the last word of your sentence.

_____   _____   _____

_____   _____   _____

_____   _____   _____

3. Write your second sentence here.

_____

4. Copy your poem here. Draw a picture to illustrate the poem.

_____

_____

by _____

Triplets and Quatrains

Older or more capable students can move from couplets to triplets and quatrains.

Triplet

A triplet is three lines that rhyme. Each line has the same number of syllables.

Up, up, up in flight
Sails my rainbow kite.
What a pretty sight.

Quatrain

A quatrain is four lines that can be written in several different rhyming patterns.

AABB—lines 1 and 2 rhyme;
lines 3 and 4 rhyme

Birthday parties are great affairs
With presents such as teddy bears.
Presents, cake, and then cool ice cream
An answer to a birthday dream.

ABCB—lines 2 and 4 rhyme;
lines 1 and 3 do not rhyme

Tiny hummingbird
Dart from flower to flower.
Rainbows in motion
In a garden bower.

ABAB—lines 1 and 3 rhyme;
lines 2 and 4 rhyme

Hear that noisy purr?
A cat with two white paws
Cleans her soft gray fur,
Her whiskers, and her claws.

ABBA—lines 1 and 4 rhyme;
lines 2 and 3 rhyme

Snowflakes are falling all around
Dancing and prancing in the air
Falling, then landing everywhere
Laying cold winter on the ground.

Cinquain

Word-Count Cinquain

A form of cinquain that is successful with younger students relies on word count rather than a strict adherence to syllable count.

Line 1—one word (title)
Line 2—two words (describe the title)
Line 3—three words (describe an action)
Line 4—four words (describe a feeling)
Line 5—one word (refer to the title)

Owl
Swift, ferocious
Watches for food
Soaring through the night
Hunter

Syllable-Count Cinquain

Traditional cinquain follows a pattern of five lines containing 22 syllables in a specific pattern.

Line 1—two syllables
Line 2—four syllables
Line 3—six syllables
Line 4—eight syllables
Line 5—two syllables

Hamsters
Furry creatures
Twitching little noses
Loving, cozy, fluffy cotton
Cuddly

Writing Cinquain

• Select the word-count or syllable-count cinquain pattern.

• Pages 13–15 present three levels of word-count cinquain writing lessons. Use the level that is most appropriate for your students.

• Pages 18–20 present three levels of syllable-count cinquain writing lessons. Use the level that is most appropriate for your students.

• After completing the Level I lesson, you may want students to copy and illustrate the poem.

Level 1

Students are guided through all of the steps to write a word-count cinquain. Here is a sample lesson.

1. Select a topic of interest to your students. List the title on a chart or the chalkboard.

puppy

2. Brainstorm and develop a list of words that describe the title.

soft   furry
floppy ears   curly tail
happy tail   black spots

3. Brainstorm and develop a list of three-word phrases that describe an action relating to the topic.

runs in circles   chasing my cat
digging for bones   wiggles in sleep
fetching a stick   follows me home

4. Brainstorm and develop a list of four-word phrases that describe a feeling experienced by or about the topic.

happy to see me
eager to play again
dreaming of lost bones
protecting his backyard
chasing his own tail
hungry for a snack

5. Brainstorm and develop a list of words that refer to the title.

dog   pet
friend   collie
companion   pal

6. The class decides on a word or phrase for each line of the cinquain.

Puppy   Puppy
Happy tail   Soft, furry
Follows me home   Wiggles in sleep
Eager to play again   Dreaming of lost bones
Pal   Pet

Writing a Word-Count Cinquain

Students are guided through steps one through five. They do step six independently. Here is a sample lesson.

1. Select a topic of interest to your students. List the title on a chart or the chalkboard.

    otter

2. Brainstorm and develop a list of words that describe the title.

    ocean mammal
    furry creature
    super swimmer
    hungry hunter

3. Brainstorm and develop a list of three-word phrases that describe an action relating to the topic.

    dives for food
    grooming baby's fur
    sleeps in kelp
    scratching its nose
    nurses her baby
    hides from danger

4. Brainstorm and develop a list of four-word phrases that describe a feeling experienced by or about the topic.

    enjoys the cool water
    loves her little one
    happy in the ocean
    frightened by loud noises

5. Brainstorm and develop a list of words that refer to the title. (Some students may choose to repeat the topic word.)

    mother
    fur ball
    clown

6. Students select a word or phrase from each step to write their own cinquains.

    Otter
    Furry creature
    Dives for food
    Enjoys the cool water
    Otter

    Otter
    Ocean mammal
    Grooming baby's fur
    Loves her little one
    Mother

Level III

Students at this level have had lots of guided practice and are ready to write word-count cinquains independently.

• Reproduce the "How to" chart on page 16 on a transparency or post it where students can refer to it while writing.

• Reproduce the step-by-step form on page 17 if students need assistance in the writing process or use any of the topic forms on pages 52–71.

• Students at this level should be guided to revise and rewrite their poems. They might work in pairs or small groups to refine the descriptive vocabulary and adherence to the poetry form. Tell students what you like about their poems *(This phrase does an excellent job of showing feelings.)*, but don't be afraid to offer suggestions for improvement *(Why don't you try some other words that rename your topic? A different word on the last line will add interest to your poem.)*.

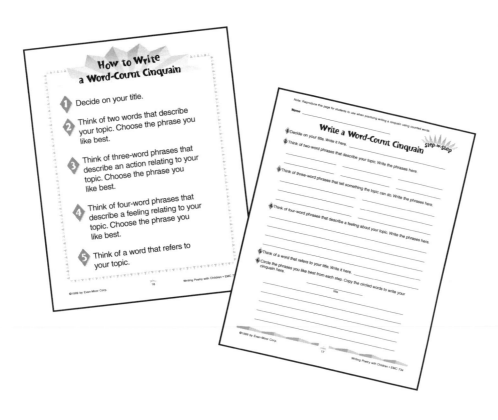

Writing Poetry with Children • EMC 734

How to Write a Word-Count Cinquain

1 Decide on your title.

2 Think of two words that describe your topic. Choose the phrase you like best.

3 Think of three-word phrases that describe an action relating to your topic. Choose the phrase you like best.

4 Think of four-word phrases that describe a feeling relating to your topic. Choose the phrase you like best.

5 Think of a word that refers to your topic.

Name _____

Write a Word-Count Cinquain
Step-by-Step

1. Decide on your title. Write it here. _____

2. Think of two-word phrases that describe your topic. Write the phrases here.

_____   _____   _____

_____   _____   _____

3. Think of three-word phrases that tell something the topic can do. Write the phrases here.

_____   _____

_____   _____

_____   _____

4. Think of four-word phrases that describe a feeling about your topic. Write the phrases here.

_____

_____

_____

_____

5. Think of a word that refers to your title. Write it here. _____

6. Circle the phrases you like best from each step. Copy the circled words to write your cinquain here.

_____
title

_____

_____

_____

_____

Writing a Syllable-Count Cinquain

Students are guided through all of the steps to write a syllable-count cinquain. Here is a sample lesson.

1. Provide a topic containing two syllables.

snowflakes

2. Brainstorm and develop a list of four-syllable words or phrases about the topic.

softly falling
icy crystals
lightly floating
cold winter lace
down toward the Earth
swirling in wind

3. Brainstorm and develop a list of six-syllable phrases about the topic.

playful winter fairies
fragile flowers of ice
forming mountains of white
make a winter playground

4. Brainstorm and develop a list of eight-syllable phrases about the topic.

looking like frozen cotton balls
filling our winter hearts with joy
shining frosting for winter trees

5. Brainstorm and create a list of two-syllable words or phrases that refer to the title.

crystals
white lace
surprise

6. As a class, select words or phrases from each list to create a cinquain. Students copy and illustrate the cinquain.

Snowflakes
Lightly floating
Down toward the Earth
Shining frosting for winter trees
White lace

Level II

Students are guided through steps one through five. They do step six independently. Encourage students to come up with an idea first, and then make adjustments to fit the correct syllable count.

1. Select a topic of interest to your students. It must contain two syllables. List the title on the chalkboard.

    dragon

2. Brainstorm and develop a list of four-syllable words or phrases about the topic

    swiftly flying
    mythical beast

3. Brainstorm and develop a list of six-syllable phrases about the topic.

    searching the land below
    shrieking as it attacks
    seeking food for dinner
    following the brave knight

4. Brainstorm and develop a list of eight-syllable phrases about the topic.

    soaring over the mountaintops
    waiting in anticipation
    shadow darkens the land below
    silent death dropping from the sky

5. Brainstorm and create a list of two-syllable words or phrases that refer to the title.

    hungry   danger
    fable   monster
    farewell   battle

6. Students write their own cinquain using the lists created by the class.

    Dragon   Dragon
    Mythical beast   Swiftly flying
    Following the brave knight   Searching the land below
    Silent death dropping from the sky   Waiting in anticipation
    Battle   Hungry

 Writing Poetry with Children • EMC 734

Writing a Syllable-Count Cinquain

Level III

Students at this level have had lots of guided practice and are ready to write syllable-count cinquains independently.

• Reproduce the "How to" chart on page 21 on a transparency or post it where students can refer to it while writing.

• Reproduce the step-by-step form on page 22 if students need assistance in the writing process or use any of the topic forms on pages 52–71.

• Students at this level should be guided to revise and rewrite their poems. They might work in pairs or small groups to refine the descriptive vocabulary and adherence to the poetry form. Tell students what you like about their poems *(You've done an excellent job of keeping the syllable count in your cinquain.)*, but don't be afraid to offer suggestions for improvement *(This line doesn't seem as strong as the rest of your poem. Why don't you try to a few other ideas to see if you come up with something you like better.)*.

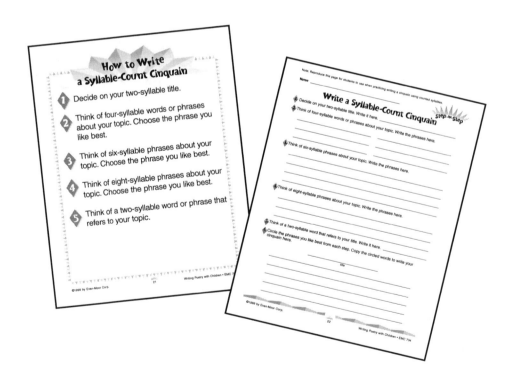

How to Write
a Syllable-Count Cinquain

1 Decide on your two-syllable title.

2 Think of four-syllable words or phrases about your topic. Choose the phrase you like best.

3 Think of six-syllable phrases about your topic. Choose the phrase you like best.

4 Think of eight-syllable phrases about your topic. Choose the phrase you like best.

5 Think of a two-syllable word or phrase that refers to your topic.

Name _____

Write a Syllable-Count Cinquain

Step-by-Step

1. Decide on your two-syllable title. Write it here. _____

2. Think of four-syllable words or phrases about your topic. Write the phrases here.

_____ _____

_____ _____

_____ _____

3. Think of six-syllable phrases about your topic. Write the phrases here.

_____

_____

_____

_____

4. Think of eight-syllable phrases about your topic. Write the phrases here.

_____

_____

_____

5. Think of a two-syllable word that refers to your title. Write it here. _____

6. Circle the phrases you like best from each step. Copy the circled words to write your cinquain here.

_____
title

_____

_____

_____

_____

_____

Haiku

Simplified Haiku

Younger students may be unable to handle the exact 17 syllables of traditional haiku, but can express a feeling within a one-sentence format. Use this simplified pattern:

where it happens...On my backyard fence
what is happening...a cat sings his lonely song
when it occurs...each hot summer night.

Traditional Haiku

A haiku poem consists of 17 unrhymed syllables organized into three lines.
Line 1—5 syllables
Line 2—7 syllables
Line 3—5 syllables

Most haiku poems refer to some element of nature. They express a moment of beauty which keeps you thinking or feeling. The most important thing to remember is that the thought should come first, and then consider adjusting the syllable count.

Little hungry frog
resting on a lily pad
dreams of careless flies.

Gentle raindrops fall.
Reflected in the puddles,
thirsty flowers drink.

One sparkling spring day
I saw a tiny spider
spin a web of silk.

Writing Haiku

- Even young students can be successful with the simplified version of haiku. By fourth grade many students will be ready to try the traditional syllable-count form.
- Pages 24–26 present three levels of simplified "where, what, when" haiku writing lessons. Use the lesson that seems most appropriate for your students.
- Pages 29–31 present three levels of traditional syllable-count writing lessons. Use the lesson that seems most appropriate for your students.
- After completing the Level I lesson, you may want students to copy and illustrate the poem.

Writing a Simplified Haiku

Students are guided through all the steps to write a simplified haiku. Here is a sample lesson.

1. Select an object from nature or a photograph of a seasonal scene to stimulate ideas. Discuss the elements in the picture. For example, a picture of waves breaking on a beach in the moonlight.

2. Brainstorm and create lists of words or phrases that tell where the action is occurring.

   beach   at the ocean
   sea   along the shoreline

3. Brainstorm and create lists of phrases that tell what is happening.

   moonlight is shining
   restless waves are moving in and out
   whitecaps glow in the moonlight
   tide is coming in

4. Brainstorm and create lists of phrases that tell when it is happening.

   in the summer
   at night
   in the moonlight
   after the sun sets
   about midnight
   each year

5. Choose a "where," a "what," and a "when" phrase to create a complete thought.

   At the beach where the moon is shining
   the restless waves are moving in and out
   on summer nights.

Level II

Students are guided through steps one through four. They do step five independently. Here is a sample lesson.

1. Select an object or photograph of an object from nature such as a caterpillar. Discuss the object to stimulate writing ideas.

2. Brainstorm and create a list of phrases that tell where the action is occurring.

   along a tiny stem
   in my father's garden
   on a shiny leaf
   among the mulberry leaves
   in the cool shade
   on the child's finger

3. Brainstorm and create a list of phrases that tell what is happening.

   little caterpillar crawls
   caterpillar nibbles at leaves
   hungry caterpillar seeks food
   caterpillar rests quietly

4. Brainstorm and create a list of phrases that tell when it occurred.

   one spring day
   on a still afternoon
   day after day
   hour after hour
   when it's time to change
   all day long

5. Students independently choose and write a "where," a "what," and a "when" phrase to create a complete thought.

   Among the mulberry leaves
   a little caterpillar nibbles leaves
   one spring day.

Writing a Simplified Haiku

Students at this level have had lots of guided practice and are ready to write "where, what, when" haikus independently.

- Reproduce the "How to" chart on page 27 on a transparency or post it where students can refer to it while writing.

- Reproduce the step-by-step form on page 28 if students need assistance in the writing process or use any of the topic forms on pages 52–71.

- Students at this level should be guided to revise and rewrite their poems. They might work in pairs or small groups to refine the descriptive vocabulary and adherence to the poetry form. Tell students what you like about their poems *(This phrase really paints a picture of what is happening.)*, but don't be afraid to offer suggestions for improvement *(Why don't you try to make this line show "time" more clearly.)*.

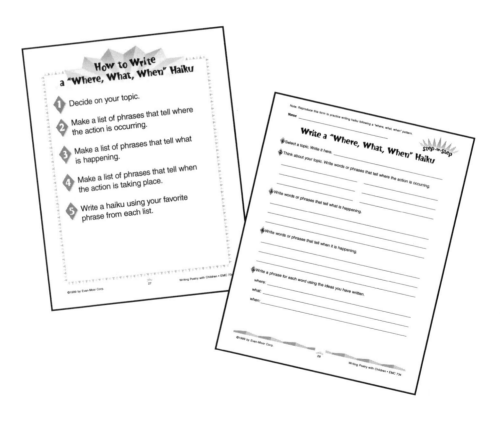

Writing a Simplified Haiku

How to Write a "Where, What, When" Haiku

1 Decide on your topic.

2 Make a list of phrases that tell where the action is occurring.

3 Make a list of phrases that tell what is happening.

4 Make a list of phrases that tell when the action is taking place.

5 Write a haiku using your favorite phrase from each list.

Name _____

Write a "Where, What, When" Haiku

1. Select a topic. Write it here. _____

2. Think about your topic. Write words or phrases that tell where the action is occurring.

_____   _____

_____   _____

_____   _____

3. Write words or phrases that tell what is happening.

_____

_____

_____

4. Write words or phrases that tell when it is happening.

_____

_____

_____

5. Write a phrase for each word using the ideas you have written.

where: _____

what: _____

when: _____

Level I

Students are guided through all the steps to write a traditional 17-syllable haiku. Here is a sample lesson.

1. Select an object from nature or a photograph of a seasonal scene to stimulate ideas. For example, have students write about some aspect of autumn.

2. Students brainstorm and create a list of words or phrases that describe the object (how it looks, feels, etc.), or words that tell how they feel about the object.

autumn	preparing for winter
cool	seasons changing
shining colors	leaves change color
trees	gold, red, yellow
winds blow	squirrels store nuts

3. As a class, write a sentence using the ideas developed in step two.

Tree, why are your leaves changing color?
Autumn is here.

4. As a class, adjust the syllable count and words to fit the haiku pattern.

Lovely willow tree,
Why are your leaves turning gold?
Autumn has arrived.

Writing a Traditional Haiku

1. Select an object from nature or a photograph of a seasonal scene to stimulate ideas. For example, have students touch pieces of bark from a tree.

2. Brainstorm and create a list of words or phrases that describe the object (how it looks, feels, etc.), or how you feel about the object.

brown   feels rough in *my* hand
deep cracks   children touch the bark
curious   bark of an old oak tree
ancient   a strange feeling

3. Independently, students select and write words and phrases from step two to create a sentence.

The bark from the ancient oak felt rough in the curious child's hand.

4. Students adjust the syllables and words of their sentences to fit the haiku pattern.

Oh, ancient oak tree
how strange *your* rugged bark felt
to curious hands.

Level III

Students at this level have had lots of guided practice and are ready to write traditional haikus independently.

• Reproduce the "How to" chart on page 32 on a transparency or post it where students can refer to it while writing.

• Reproduce the step-by-step form on page 33 if students need assistance in the writing process or use any of the topic forms on pages 52–71.

• Students at this level should be guided to revise and rewrite their poems. They might work in pairs or small groups to refine the descriptive vocabulary and adherence to the poetry form. Tell students what you like about their poems *(Your excellent use of adjectives really helps me see this season in my mind.),* but don't be afraid to offer suggestions for improvement *(Can you think of a one-syllable word to use here to make your syllable count correct?).*

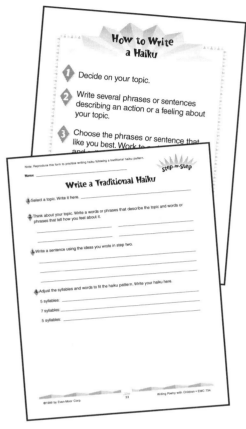

Note:

Even famous haiku poets weren't slaves to specific line-syllable count. In this verse, Buson retained 17 syllables for the verse, but not a 5–7–5 count.

Sweet spring shower...
Enough to wet the tiny shells
On this little beach.
Buson

Writing Poetry with Children • EMC 734

How to Write a Haiku

 **1** Decide on your topic.

2 Write several phrases or sentences describing an action or a feeling about your topic.

3 Choose the phrases or sentence that like you best. Work to make the words and syllables fit the correct haiku form.

5 syllables
7 syllables
5 syllables

Note: Reproduce this form to practice writing haiku following a traditional haiku pattern.

Name _____

step-by-step

Write a Traditional Haiku

1. Select a topic. Write it here. _____

2. Think about your topic. Write a words or phrases that describe the topic and words or phrases that tell how you feel about it.

_____   _____

_____   _____

3. Write a sentence using the ideas you wrote in step two.

_____

_____

_____

4. Adjust the syllables and words to fit the haiku pattern. Write your haiku here.

5 syllables: _____

7 syllables: _____

5 syllables: _____

Limericks

A limerick is an amusing verse of five lines. Lines 1, 2, and 5 rhyme and lines 3 and 4 rhyme. Line 5 refers to line 1. Lines 3 and 4 are usually shorter than the other lines.

Limericks follow a specific rhythm pattern. Although adherence to a strict rhythm should not be expected, students will get a "feel" for it if you share lots of limericks aloud.

There once was a musical king
Who suddenly started to sing.
    The birds in the sky
    All started to fly
Right over that talented king.

There once was a student named Sam
Who loved peanut butter and jam.
    This snack is the best
    It tops all the rest
Reported that fellow named Sam.

Writing Limericks

- The limerick form is too difficult for most primary students. It can be successful with more able third graders with much guidance.

- Read limericks aloud to your students to demonstrate the limerick rhythm and rhyming pattern. (See the bibliography on page 96.)

- Pages 35–37 present three levels of limerick writing lessons. Use the lesson that seems most appropriate for your students.

- After completing the Level I lesson, you may want students to copy and illustrate the limerick.

- Allow students having difficulty with the format to work with a partner or in a small group.

Level 1

1. Provide lines 1, 2, and 5.

Line 1—Today when my favorite clown
Line 2—Arrived he was wearing a frown

Line 5— "I'm getting a new job in town."

2. Brainstorm and create a list of possible ideas to fit into lines 3 and 4. Don't worry about rhyming at this point.

tired of falling
slip on a peel
pie in the face
laughed at each day
stuffed in a car
going from place to place

3. Select the line or lines your students like best. Work with the words from two short rhyming sentences.

"I'm tired of the way
I'm laughed at each day."

"No more pies in the face.
It's just a rat race."

4. Write the complete limerick using the students' favorite short lines.

Today when my favorite clown
Arrived he was wearing a frown.
"I'm tired of the way
I'm laughed at each day.
I'm getting a new job in town."

Writing Limericks

1. Guide your students through lines 1, 2, and 3.

Line 1—Brainstorm and complete the first line to tell the subject of the limerick.

There once was a _____
named _____.

There once was a fellow named Matt.

Line 2—Brainstorm and create a list of words that rhyme with the final word in line 1.

hat   bat   sat   drat
cat   rat   flat   scat

Write a second line that tells something about the subject. The second line must rhyme with the first line.

Who found something strange in his hat.
Whose pet was a big striped cat.
Who discovered his bike tire was flat.

Students decide which line they prefer.

There once was a fellow named Matt
Who found something strange in his hat.

Line 5—At this point, write the fifth line that refers to line 1.

Astonished that poor fellow named Matt.

2. Students create their own short couplets for lines 3 and 4.

3. Each student copies the lines created together, adds his or her individual couplet for lines 3 and 4, and illustrates the completed limerick.

There once was a boy named Matt
Who found something strange in his hat.
    Six pennies, some slime,
    And a story in rhyme,
Astonished that poor boy named Matt.

Students at this level have had lots of guided practice and are ready to write limericks independently.

• Reproduce the "How to" chart on page 38 on a transparency or post it where students can refer to it while writing.

• Reproduce the step-by-step form on page 39 if students need assistance in the writing process or use any of the topic forms on pages 52–71.

• Students at this level should be guided to revise and rewrite their poems. They might work in pairs or small groups to refine the descriptive vocabulary and adherence to the poetry form. Tell students what you like about their poems *(Your limerick is so funny I laughed out loud when I read it.),* but don't be afraid to offer suggestions for improvement *(Your first line and last line are the same. This is one way to end a limerick. But I'll bet someone as creative as you can think of a different ending. How about giving it a try?).*

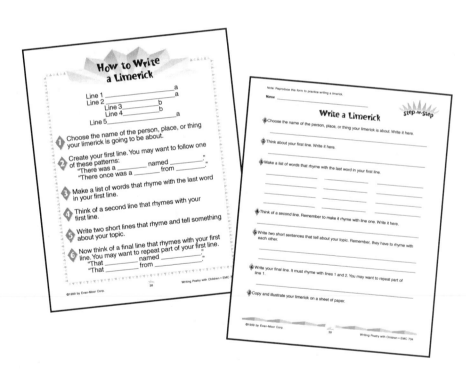

Writing Limericks

How to Write a Limerick

Line 1 _____ a
Line 2 _____ a
      Line 3_____ b
      Line 4_____ b
Line 5_____ a

1 Choose the name of the person, place, or thing your limerick is going to be about.

2 Create your first line. You may want to follow one of these patterns:
"There was a _____ named _____."
"There once was a _____ from _____."

3 Make a list of words that rhyme with the last word in your first line.

4 Think of a second line that rhymes with your first line.

5 Write two short lines that rhyme and tell something about your topic.

6 Now think of a final line that rhymes with your first line. You may want to repeat part of your first line.
"That _____ named _____."
"That _____ from _____."

Note: Reproduce this form to practice writing a limerick.

Name _____

Write a Limerick

1. Choose the name of the person, place, or thing your limerick is about. Write it here.

_____

2. Think about your first line. Write it here.

_____

3. Make a list of words that rhyme with the last word in your first line.

_____   _____   _____

_____   _____   _____

_____   _____   _____

_____   _____   _____

4. Think of a second line. Remember to make it rhyme with line one. Write it here.

_____

5. Write two short sentences that tell about your topic. Remember, they have to rhyme with each other.

_____

_____

6. Write your final line. It must rhyme with lines 1 and 2. You may want to repeat part of line 1.

_____

7. Copy and illustrate your limerick on a sheet of paper.

Shape Poems

Sometimes it is fun to play with words in unusual ways to create a poem. Shape poems provide an opportunity for this type of experience at any grade level.

A shape poem follows the outline of a picture of the poem's subject.

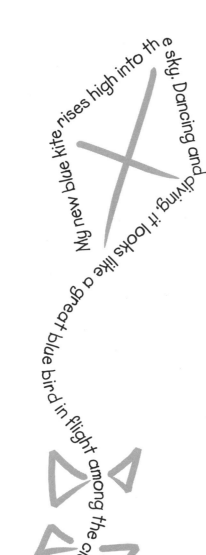

Writing Shape Poems

- While even very young writers can be successful writing shape poems, less coordinated younger students may need some help writing the poem around the shape.

- Pages 41–43 present three levels of shape poem writing lessons. Use the lesson that seems most appropriate for your students.

- Pages 72–76 contain reproducible forms students can use for additional practice.

Level 1

Students are guided through all steps to write a shape poem. Here is a sample lesson.

1. Select a topic.

   sun

2. Brainstorm and list words or phrases about the topic.

sun	warm	warms the earth
yellow	sun rays	helps flowers grow
hot	bright	makes me hot
		rays reach out

3. As a class, choose the best words and phrases and arrange them to create a pleasing sound.

   Sun, warm, yellow, rays reach out, helps flowers grow.

4. Students draw the outline of a sun, using black crayon or marking pen. They clip a sheet of thin white paper over the drawing and then write the words or phrases following the shape of the picture. Have them add "hot" to all the sun's rays. (Students may need to write an additional phrase or repeat part of the poem to complete the shape.)

Sun, warm, yellow, rays reach out, helps flowers grow. hot hot hot hot hot hot hot hot hot hot hot hot hot hot hot hot hot hot hot hot hot hot hot hot hot hot hot hot hot hot hot hot hot hot hot hot hot hot hot hot

Writing Poetry with Children • EMC 734

Writing Shape Poems

Writing Shape Poems

Students are guided through steps one and two. They do steps three and four independently. Here is a sample lesson.

1. Select a topic.

   kitten

2. Brainstorm and list words or phrases about the topic.

small	wiggly tail
purrs	sensitive whiskers
pink tongue	chases birds and mice
soft fur	hides in a flower pot
sharp claws	curls up in my lap

3. Have students choose the words and phrases they like best and arrange them to create a pleasing sound.

   my small cat purrs as she curls up in my lap, she licks her soft fur with a pink tongue, she jumps down to chase a bird

   purring kitten cleans her soft fur with a small pink tongue, hides in a flower pot on hot days, watches the birds while only her tail moves

4. Students draw the outline of a kitten, using black crayon or marking pen. They clip a sheet of thin white paper over the drawing and then write words and phrases following the shape of the picture.

5. Have students paste their poems to sheets of colored paper to frame their shape poems.

Level III

Students at this level have had lots of guided practice and are ready to write shape poems independently.

• Reproduce the "How to" chart on page 44 on a transparency or post it where students can refer to it while writing.

• Reproduce the step-by-step form on page 45 if students need assistance in the writing process or use any of the topic forms on pages 72–76.

• Students at this level should be guided to revise and rewrite their poems. They might work in pairs or small groups to refine the descriptive vocabulary and adherence to the poetry form. Tell students what you like about their poems *(It was very clever of you to make your shape poem in such an interesting pattern.)*, but don't be afraid to offer suggestions for improvement *(Your words are pretty far apart. This makes it difficult to see the shape of your poem. Why don't you see if you can think of another sentence to add to the verse and copy it over. I think you will be more satisfied with your picture.)*.

Writing Shape Poems

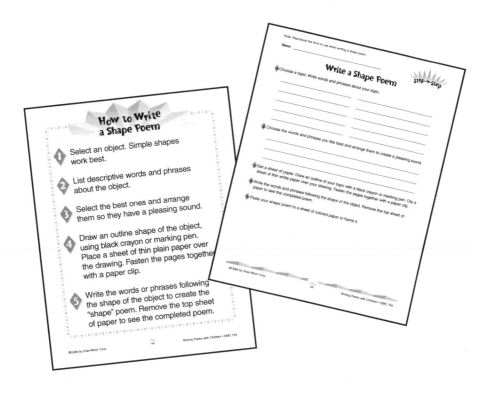

How to Write a Shape Poem

1 Select an object. Simple shapes work best.

2 List descriptive words and phrases about the object.

3 Select the best ones and arrange them so they have a pleasing sound.

4 Draw an outline shape of the object, using black crayon or marking pen. Place a sheet of thin plain paper over the drawing. Fasten the pages together with a paper clip.

5 Write the words or phrases following the shape of the object to create the "shape" poem. Remove the top sheet of paper to see the completed poem.

Name _____

Write a Shape Poem

1. Choose a topic. Write words and phrases about your topic.

_____   _____

_____   _____

_____   _____

_____   _____

_____   _____

2. Choose the words and phrases you like best and arrange them to create a pleasing sound.

_____

_____

_____

3. Get a sheet of paper. Draw an outline of your topic with a black crayon or marking pen. Clip a sheet of thin white paper over your drawing. Fasten the pages together with a paper clip.

4. Write the words and phrases following the shape of the object. Remove the top sheet of paper to see the completed poem.

5. Paste your shape poem to a sheet of colored paper to frame it.

Acrostic Poems

Another enjoyable form of word play is to create an acrostic poem. In this format, the selected topic is one word. Each word or phrase of the poem begins with a letter in the topic word. An added benefit is that students may be motivated to use a dictionary or thesaurus to help write their poems.

Read examples of acrostic poems to students before asking them to write their own. A good source of examples is *Autumn, An Alphabet Acrostic* by Steven Schnur (see bibliography, page 96).

Dashing
Over
Ground

Lovely
Even
After
Falling

Next to each other
Eggs wait under the hen
Soon little chicks will
Tap their way out

Nestled
In
Granny's bed
How nice to sleep
'**T**il morning

Writing Acrostic Poems

• This verse form seems easy at first glance, but requires a great deal of careful thinking to create a poem that makes sense.

• Stick to three-letter words when working with younger students. Even older students should not try to do more than four- or five-letter words unless they have had a great deal of experience.

• Pages 47–49 present three levels of acrostic writing lessons. Use the lesson that seems most appropriate for your students.

Level 1

Students are guided through all the steps to write an acrostic poem. Here is a sample lesson.

1. Select a word.

   cat

2. Brainstorm and list words or short phrases that describe or relate to the topic word. Remember to include words beginning with each letter in the word.

   cute   about
   clever   around
   curious   angry
   caught in the act   after a mouse
   clawing the door   a bundle of fur
                           always

   trouble
   thinking
   the house
   to reach the bird
   top of the tree

3. Write the word vertically.

   C
   A
   T

4. As a class, select one word or phrase from the list that starts with each letter of the word. Your goal is to create a descriptive phrase or sentence that has a pleasing sound. Write the word or phrase after the appropriate letter. Students copy and illustrate the poem.

   Curious
   Always in
   Trouble

   Caught in the
   Act of opening
   The birdcage door

Writing Acrostic Poems

1. Select a word.

snow

2. Brainstorm and list words or short phrases that describe or relate to the topic word. Remember to include words beginning with each letter in the topic word.

soft	new
slushy	nestle
smooth	noiseless
sparkling brightly	near the pine tree

ooze	white
out	winter
of	wonderful
over everything	wild winds blow

3. Students write the topic word down on a sheet of paper. Make the letters dark.

S _____

N _____

O _____

W _____

4. Working independently, each student selects a word or phrase from the list for each letter of the word to create a descriptive phrase or sentence that has a pleasing sound. Students write the word or phrase after the appropriate letter.

Softly	Sparkling brightly
Nestles	Near the pine tree
Over	Over every branch as
Winter	Wild winter winds blow

5. Students illustrate their poems.

Level III

Students at this level have had lots of guided practice and are ready to write acrostic poems independently.

• Reproduce the "How to" chart on page 50 on a transparency or post it where students can refer to it while writing.

• Reproduce the step-by-step form on page 51 if students need assistance in the writing process or use any of the topic forms on pages 77–81.

• Students at this level should be guided to revise and rewrite their poems. They might work in pairs or small groups to refine the descriptive vocabulary and adherence to the poetry form. Tell students what you like about their poems *(You've done a great job of telling a short story using the letters of your word.)*, but don't be afraid to offer suggestions for improvement *(You have a good beginning here. Why don't you use the dictionary to find a few more words that begin with this letter. I think that will help you finish your poem more easily.).*

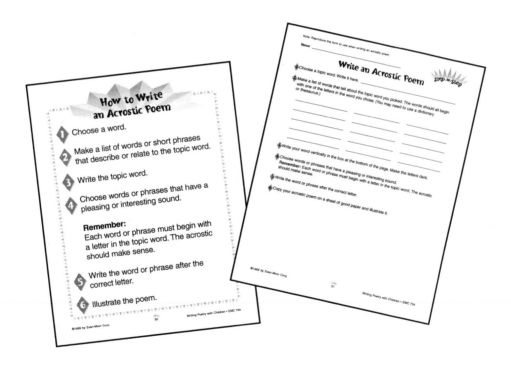

How to Write an Acrostic Poem

1 Choose a word.

2 Make a list of words or short phrases that describe or relate to the topic word.

3 Write the topic word.

4 Choose words or phrases that have a pleasing or interesting sound.

Remember:

Each word or phrase must begin with a letter in the topic word. The acrostic should make sense.

5 Write the word or phrase after the correct letter.

6 Illustrate the poem.

Name _____

Write an Acrostic Poem

◆1. Choose a topic word. Write it here. _____

◆2. Make a list of words that tell about the topic word you picked. The words should all begin with one of the letters in the word you chose. (You may need to use a dictionary or thesaurus.)

_____   _____   _____

_____   _____   _____

_____   _____   _____

_____   _____   _____

◆3. Write your word vertically in the box at the bottom of the page. Make the letters dark.

◆4. Choose words or phrases that have a pleasing or interesting sound.
    Remember: Each word or phrase must begin with a letter in the topic word. The acrostic should make sense.

◆5. Write the word or phrase after the correct letter.

◆6. Copy your acrostic poem on a sheet of good paper and illustrate it.

The Sun

by _____

_____

_____

_____

_____

Writing Poetry with Children • EMC 734

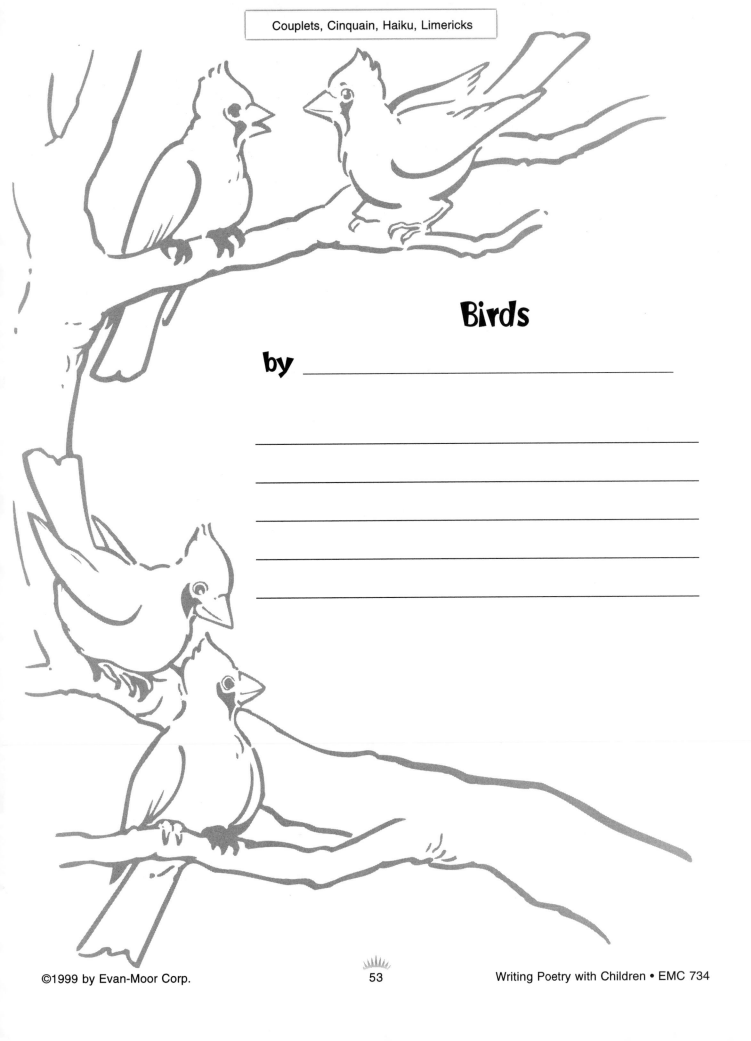

Birds

by _____

_____

_____

_____

_____

_____

Rain

by _____

_____

_____

_____

_____

_____

Writing Poetry with Children • EMC 734

A Clown

by _____

_____

_____

_____

_____

_____

The Old Car

by _____

_____

_____

_____

_____

_____

Writing Poetry with Children • EMC 734

A Butterfly

by _____

_____

_____

_____

_____

_____

Writing Poetry with Children • EMC 734

Bubbles

by _____

_____

_____

_____

_____

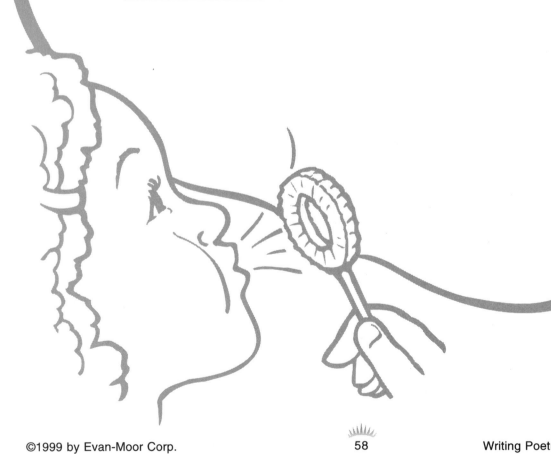

Writing Poetry with Children • EMC 734

A Spaceship

by _____

_____

_____

_____

_____

_____

Kittens

by _____

_____

_____

_____

_____

_____

Writing Poetry with Children • EMC 734

Motorcycle

by _____

_____

_____

_____

_____

_____

Willow Tree

by _____

_____

_____

_____

_____

The Storm

by _____

_____

_____

_____

_____

_____

Cricket

by _____

_____

_____

_____

_____

_____

Fireflies

by _____

Winter

by _____

_____

_____

_____

_____

_____

Bat

by _____

_____

_____

_____

_____

_____

An Old Man with a Beard

by _____

_____

_____

_____

_____

The Knight

by _____

_____

_____

_____

_____

Cowboy

by _____

_____

_____

_____

_____

_____

Space Alien

by _____

_____

_____

_____

_____

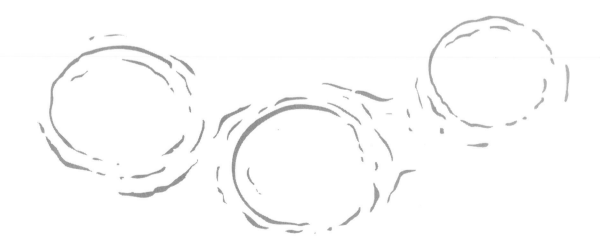

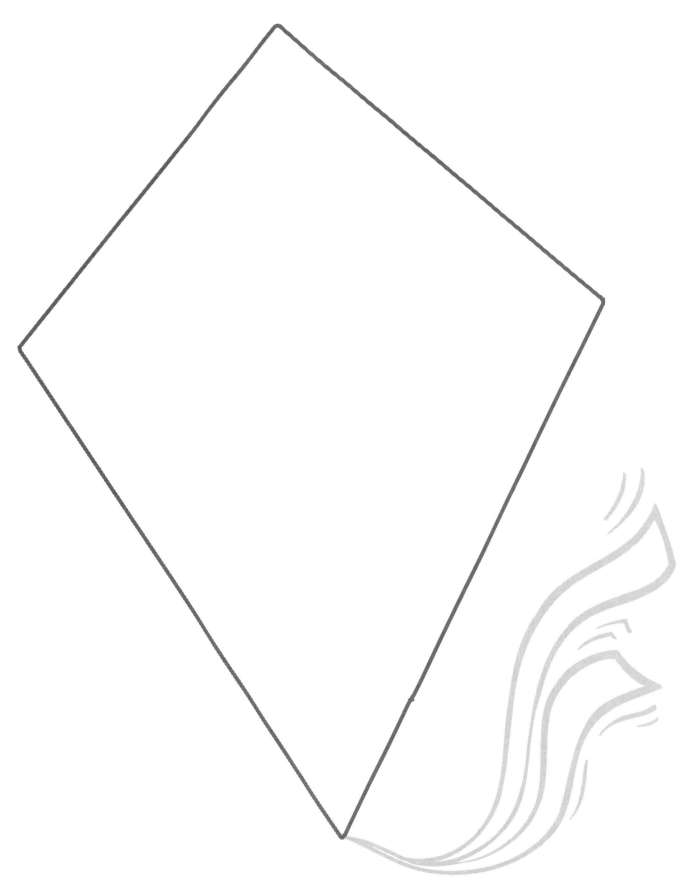

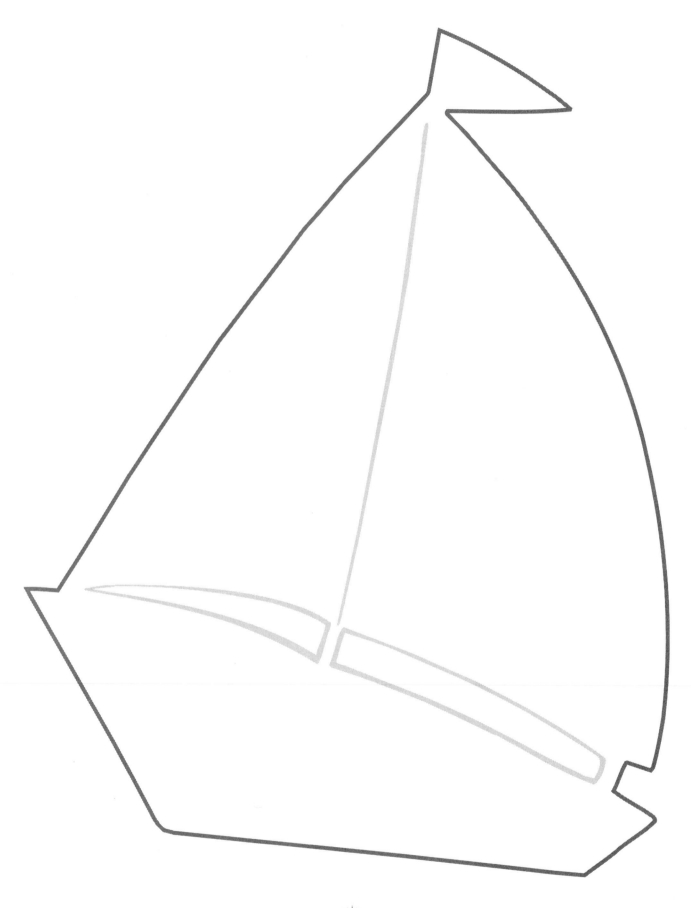

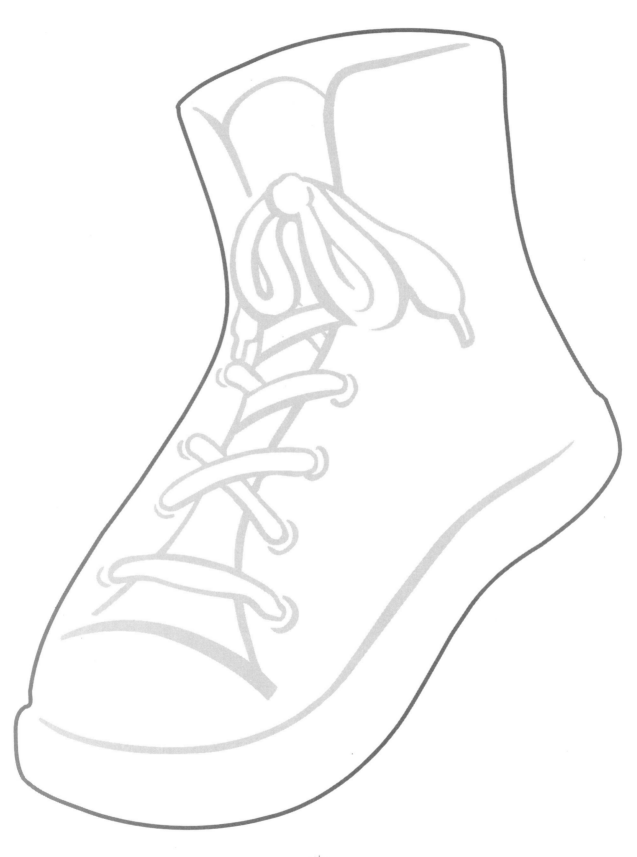

Writing Poetry with Children • EMC 734

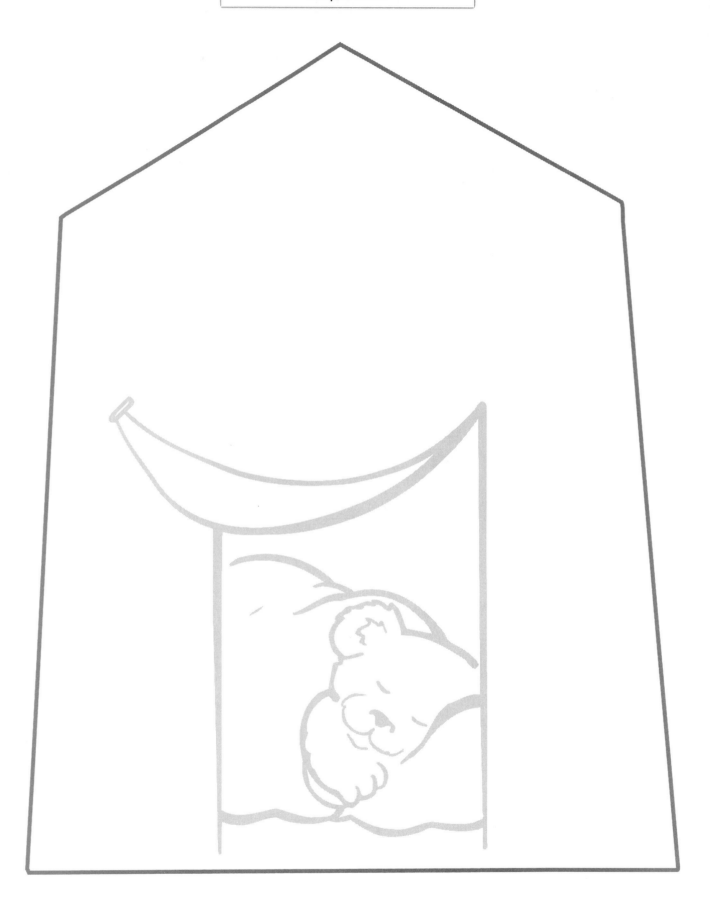

Frog

by _____

F _____

R _____

O _____

G _____

Rain

by _____

R _____

A _____

I _____

N _____

Star

by _____

S _____

T _____

A _____

R _____

Writing Poetry with Children • EMC 734

Ocean

by _____

O _____

C _____

E _____

A _____

N _____

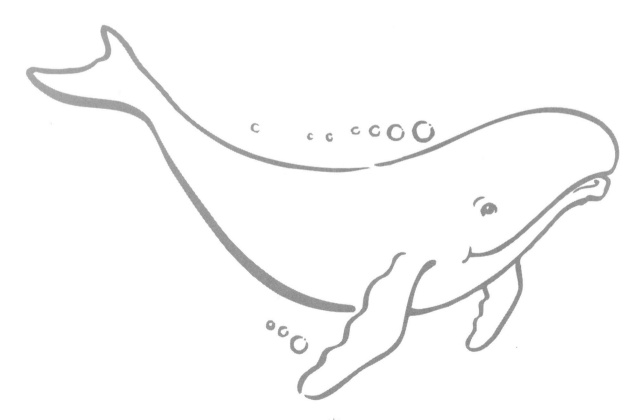

Writing Poetry with Children • EMC 734

Home

by _____

H _____

O _____

M _____

E _____

Writing Poetry with Children • EMC 734

Potpourri of Poetry Writing Ideas

After your students have been exposed to a variety of poetry forms, provide opportunities for practice using their favorites. Pages 82–84 contain several writing experiences where students can use the poetry forms they have practiced.

Rewrite Old Favorites

Nursery Rhymes
Read a favorite nursery rhyme. Discuss the form in which it is written. If there is an obvious pattern, write an outline on the chalkboard. Students select new topics to write about using the pattern.

(Twinkle, Twinkle, Little Star)

Flicker, flicker little light
Shining brightly in the night.
Orange and round overhead
Like the night-light near my bed.
Flicker, flicker little light
Shining brightly in the night.

(Baa, Baa, Black Sheep)

Buzz, buzz, yellow bee
Have you any honey?
Yes sir, yes sir,
I sell it for money.
1 jar is a nickel,
2 jars are a dime.
Come along and
Buy some anytime.

Fairy Tales
This activity is for older, more able students. Select a short version of a favorite fairy tale. Have students agree on the poetry form to use for the rewrite. Assign a story section to a student (or small group) to rewrite in verse. Compile the completed sections in sequence and bind into a book.

A frightful troll
(With a big brown mole)
    Lives under the bridge nearby.
He wouldn't permit
Anyone to cross it
    But the goats decided to try.

Three Gruff goats
(With hairy coats)
    Lived on the side of a hill.
They nibbled grass seeds
And tasty green weeds
    Like clover, wild oats, and dill.

Describe Yourself

Review the various poetry forms your students have learned. Students list words and phrases that describe themselves. They then select one or more verse forms to use in writing the descriptions of themselves.

(Couplet)
My name is Jimmy Lee.
I have a fun hobby.

I collect license plates
From all the fifty states.

(Cinquain)
Aimee
Tall, freckles
Paints beautiful pictures
Laughs at funny jokes
Me

(Acrostic)
Kind and friendly
Always busy
Takes gymnastics
You'll like me

Holiday Poems

Review the various poetry forms your students have learned. Brainstorm and create a list of words and phrases about a holiday. Students write about the holiday in two or more different poetry styles.

(Couplet)
My friend Tommy gave me a fright
When I saw him Halloween night.

(Cinquain)
Night
Quiet darkness
Children move about
Shivers and excited giggles
Halloween

(Haiku)
A still autumn night
Excited child creeps about—
Halloween has come.

Alphabet Book

Review the couplet form. Brainstorm and make lists of words that rhyme with each letter of the alphabet. Assign a letter to each student. The student is to write and illustrate a couplet about that letter. Arrange the pages in alphabetical order and place into a cover.

The letter A
Rests on hay

While letter B
Floats in the sea

And letter C
Chases a bee

Counting Book

Review the couplet form. Brainstorm and list items that might be used in the counting book and words that rhyme with those items. Assign a number to each student or pair of students. Students write and illustrate a couplet about their number. Arrange the pages in numerical order and place into a cover.

1 One lazy cat
Napped in a hat.

2 Two funny ants
Were wearing pants.

3 Three chicks in a nest
Took a little rest.

4 Four hairy goats
Floated in boats.

5 A swarm of five bees
Flew around the trees.

One lazy cat
Napped in a hat.

Writing Poetry with Children • EMC 734

Poetry Writing Center

Create a center containing task cards and an assortment of types of paper and writing implements.

1. Place a table in front of a small bulletin board. Cover the bulletin board in colorful butcher paper and add a title using a broad-tipped marker or letters cut from contrasting paper.

2. Use small manila envelopes to make pockets to hold the task cards. Glue one copy of each task to the front of an envelope. (Select the task cards that are appropriate for your students.) Put several copies of each writing task in the envelopes. Pin the envelopes to the bulletin board.

3. Place paper, pencils, pens, marking pens, etc., on the table.

4. Students will select a task card and then write the type of poem described on the card.

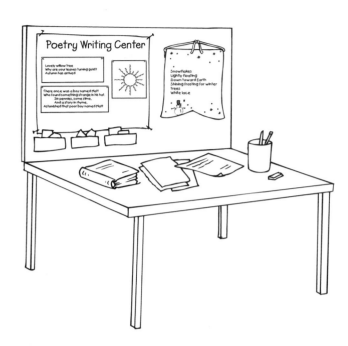

Think about your favorite snack. Write a poem about how it looks, smells, and tastes.

Make a wish for yourself (or someone else) in rhyme.

85

Make a list of words and sounds you enjoy. Arrange some of the words on your list into an order that creates your favorite kind of poem.

Write an acrostic using the name of one of these:
a. your favorite animal
b. a super hero
c. a character from a book

Write a riddle in rhyme.

Follow this pattern to write a poem. The two lines must rhyme.

The _____ is as _____
As _____ _____.

Write a poem that will make someone laugh out loud.

Rewrite one or more verses of your favorite song using the same rhyming pattern but a different subject.

Write a poem that shows someone how you feel when you are _____.

angry
lonely
happy

sad
embarrassed
frightened

Create a lovely (or funny) verse card for a _____.

Valentine
Birthday
Kwanzaa
Thank-you

Christmas
Easter
Hanukkah
I'm Sorry
Congratulations

Displaying Student-Authored Poems

Display Boards

If you plan to do a great deal of poetry writing during the school year, you may want to set aside one bulletin board area just for displaying your students' original writings.

Cover a bulletin board with butcher paper. Add a heading cut from colorful construction paper. Mount poems on construction paper. Pin poems to the board. Change the poems frequently.

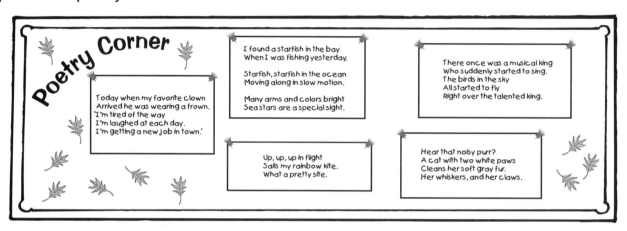

Charts and Banners

Display your students' original poetry on banners or charts. Older students can copy and illustrate their own. Younger students may need an adult's help in printing large enough letters. They can make their own decorations. Hang the banners or charts on a bulletin board or a chart rack so that students can share each other's work.

An easy banner can be made using a 12" x 24" (30.5 x 61 cm) piece of butcher paper and a 30" (76 cm) piece of yarn. Fold the top of the paper under twice, about 1" (2.5 cm) each time. Place the yarn under the fold and glue the fold down. Tie the ends of the yarn together. Write the poem on the banner using marking pens.

Sharing Student-Authored Poems

One of the best ways to motivate your students to write poetry is to provide many opportunities for sharing their finished work.

Newsletter

Once a month (quarter, semester, etc.), send home a newsletter containing students' original poetry created during that period. Use the newsletter form on page 90 or help your students create their own format. (You may want to scan page 90 to make a computer newsletter template.)

Program

Invite parents and other interested parties to a spring program where students recite their own (or classmates') poetry. (Some students will prefer to recite with a group.) This doesn't need to be a complicated process. Students sitting in groups on the stage floor or on stools can be as effective as elaborate staging and costumes. Punch and cookies afterwards gives everyone a chance to get better acquainted (and to pass around compliments to your young poets). Have students create an invitation and program form or reproduce the ones on pages 91 and 92.

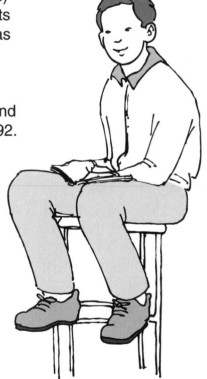

_____

newsletter title

issue number _____   **date** _____

Writing Poetry with Children • EMC 734

_____

proudly presents

_____

_____

Join us to hear original poetry written by our class this year.

Time: _____

Place: _____

Please join us!

_____

_____

presented by _____

poem	author	recited by
_____	_____	_____
_____	_____	_____
_____	_____	_____
_____	_____	_____
_____	_____	_____
_____	_____	_____
_____	_____	_____
_____	_____	_____
_____	_____	_____

Writing Poetry with Children • EMC 734

Collecting Student-Authored Poems

Portfolios

Use an art period near the beginning of the school year to create individual portfolios in which to save original poetry. These can be as simple as large manila envelopes decorated with marking pens or crayons. They may be elaborate portfolios made from butcher paper or tagboard decorated with collages or block printing and tied with yarn or ribbon.

As the year progresses, students save their poetry in their portfolios. When you are ready to create newsletters or class books, students will have a nice selection from which to choose. It is exciting for students to see how much their writing improves over a period of time.

Poetry Books

Putting books written and illustrated by your students into a class library is an excellent way to collect and to share students' original poetry. Follow these steps for putting a book together:

1. Create pages.

2. Attach poem pages.
   Pages may be stapled together before being put into a cover.

   Pages may be glued to a backing of construction paper, and then stapled together and put into a cover.

   Pages may be folded in half, and then glued back-to-back.

   Pages may be folded, and then stitched down the center. Stitching may be done by machine or by hand with darning needles.

3. Create covers (see page 94).

Book-Binding Techniques

Covers can be made from many different materials.

mat board	cardboard
construction paper	wallpaper
tagboard	cloth

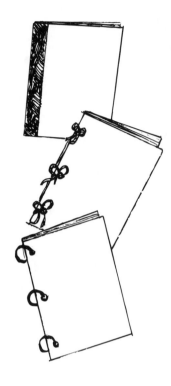

- **Quick and Easy Covers**
  1. Staple cover to pages. Cover the staples with a strip of colored tape.

  2. Lace cover to pages. Punch holes through the cover and pages. Tie them together with shoelaces, yarn, or string.
     a. down through end holes
     b. up through middle hole
     c. tie on top

  3. Use rings to hold the book together. Punch one or more holes through the cover and pages. Attach metal rings.

- **Hinged Covers**

  Cut two pieces of cover material slightly larger than the poetry pages.

  Cut 1/2" (1.25 cm) strip from the left-hand side of the front cover.

  Tape the strips together on the inside. Leave a small space open between the two strips.

  Staple the cover and poetry pages together. Cover the front hinge and staples and the back staples with a 1 1/2" (3.75 cm) strip of tape.

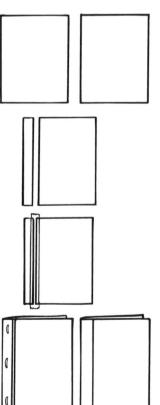

Using Poetry to Teach Skills

Use poetry to add interest to practicing skills in a variety of academic areas.

- **Practice Memory Skills**
  Even very young students can memorize short poems such as simple couplets and nursery rhymes. Older students can memorize whole poems with several stanzas. You might:
    teach a poem to the whole class each week
    assign one stanza of a long poem to different individuals or small groups
    have each student in class memorize a poem for a class poetry recital

- **Develop Concepts**
  Look in poetry anthologies to find poems that contain historical or scientific information pertinent to topics being studied.

- **Practice Comprehension**
  Poetry can be used to recall information, draw conclusions, or make inferences. Students can also sequence words, phrases, sentences, or stanzas of a poem.

- **Develop a Richer Vocabulary**
  Good poetry exposes students to rich language. Use poetry to:
    show new ways of using familiar words
    teach the meaning of new words
    search for opposites, rhyming words, synonyms, etc.
    find the nouns, verbs, adjectives, etc.
    find metaphors and similes
    look for uses of alliteration
    appreciate the beauty of language

- **Critical Thinking**
  Older students can use poems to compare and contrast:
    two poems on the same topic, but written in different poetry forms
    two poems by different authors written in the same style
    two poems by the same poet written in different styles

- **Stimulate Use of the Dictionary and Thesaurus**
  Students with adequate reading skills will be motivated to use a dictionary or thesaurus as they write poems in different styles.

95   Writing Poetry with Children • EMC 734

Bibliography

A Light in the Attic by Shel Silverstein; HarperCollins, 1981.

A. Nonny Mouse Writes Again! edited by Jack Prelutsky; Dragonfly, 1996.

Antarctic Antics: A Book of Penguin Poems by Judy Sierra; Harcourt Brace, 1998.

The Arnold Lobel Book of Mother Goose edited by Arnold Lobel; Knopf, 1997.

Autumn: An Alphabet Acrostic by Steven Schnur; Clarion Books,1997.

Beast Feast by Douglas Florian; Harcourt Brace, 1994.

The Beauty of the Beast: Poems from the Animal Kingdom edited by Jack Prelutsky;
    Knopf, 1997.

The Classic Mother Goose edited by Armand Eisen; Courage Books, 1997.

Click, Rumble, Roar: Poems about Machines edited by Lee Bennett Hopkins;
    Harpercrest, 1987.

Cricket Never Does: A Collection of Haiku and Tanka by Myra Cohn Livingston;
    Margaret McElderry, 1997.

Daffy Down Dillies: Silly Limericks by Edward Lear; Boyds Mills Press, 1992.

Falling Up: Poems and Drawings by Shel Silverstein; HarperCollins, 1996.

Hiawatha by Henry Wadsworth Longfellow; Puffin, 1996.

Hiawatha's Childhood by Henry Wadsworth Longfellow; Farrar, Straus & Giroux, 1984.

In the Eyes of the Cat: Japanese Poetry for All Seasons by Demi; Henry Holt, 1994.

Knock at a Star by X. M. Kennedy & Dorothy M. Kennedy; Little, Brown & Company, 1985.

Mother Goose by Michael Hague; Henry Holt & Company, 1988.

The New Kid on the Block by Jack Prelutsky; Greenwillow, 1994.

Oh, A-Hunting We Will Go by John Langstaff; Aladdin Paperbacks, 1991. (Couplets)

The Oxford Book of Children's Verse in America edited by Donald Hall; Oxford University
    Press, 1990.

Paul Revere's Ride by Henry Wadsworth Longfellow; Puffin, 1996.

Poems Have Roots by Lilian Moore; Atheneum, 1997.

The Random House Book of Poetry for Children selected by Jack Prelutsky; Random
    Library, 1987.

Ring of Earth by Jane Yolen; Harcourt Brace, 1986.

Spring: A Haiku Story by George Shannon; Greenwillow, 1996.

Stopping by Woods on a Snowy Evening by Robert Frost; Puffin, 1998.

Table of Contents

About the Stories

Through biographies and realistic fiction, students will learn about people, events, and ideas that represent the grand diversity of the people of North America.

While providing reading practice, the 22 stories in *Read and Understand, Celebrating Diversity, Grades 1–2* present ideas and information that address diversity objectives in current standards outlined by the National Council for the Social Studies.

The stories in this book progress from first- to low third-grade reading levels. When dealing with biographies and social studies content, certain specific vocabulary is necessary. For this reason, the readability of some of the stories in this book may be at a higher level than students can read independently.

How to Use the Stories

We suggest that you use the stories in this book for shared and guided reading experiences. Prior to reading, be sure to introduce any vocabulary that students may find difficult to decode or understand. A list of suggested words to teach is given on pages 3 and 4.

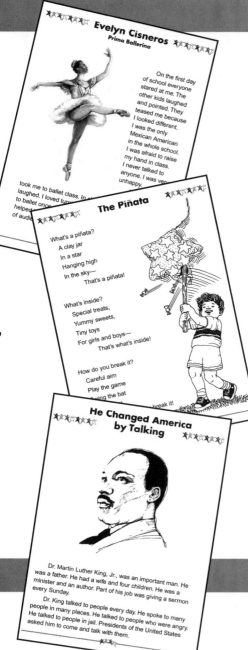

Each story is followed by four pages of activities covering specific reading skills:

- comprehension
- vocabulary
- making connections to students' own lives—comparison, evaluation, feelings
- making connections to the curriculum—mathematics, geography, written language, etc.

Vocabulary to Teach

The content of the stories in *Read and Understand, Celebrating Diversity, Grades 1–2* requires that specific vocabulary be used. This vocabulary is often at a higher level than might be expected for these grade levels. We suggest, therefore, that you introduce these words to your students before presenting the story. Read the story to pinpoint additional words they may not know.

Count with Us 5
different, languages, Japanese, Spanish, Arabic, cousin, German

The Game 12
goal, yard, cheer, believe

The Piñata 18
piñata, Mexico, United States, special, careful

My Dad's Warehouse 24
warehouse, clerks, catalogs, labels, orders, member, important

How to Use Chopsticks 30
chopsticks

Two Ways to Remember 36
scrapbook, Nhia, Thailand, Colorado, America, China, memories, remembering, stitches, bamboo, journey

My Granny's Bread 43
lefse, dough, griddle, spatula, sausage, lutefisk, lye, Norway

Jim Abbott, Baseball Pitcher 49
Jim Abbott, determined, pitcher, major-league, Little League, Pan-American Games, Olympics, California Angels, big-league, handicapped, practiced, rookie

How Does It Grow? 55
paddies, kernels, irrigated, ditches, stalks, Oscar, Sylvie, grains, sways, ripe, Celine, harvest, breeze

Susan Butcher, A Champion 62
Susan Butcher, champion, Alaska, Anchorage, Nome, Iditarod, ford, Bering Sea, Massachusetts, Maine, Fairbanks, Alaska, huskies, musher, snowshoes, solitary, calendar, temperature, remote, husband

Running to Fame 68
Jesse Owens, Alabama, sharecroppers, Ohio, college, Charles Riley, Olympics

Evelyn Cisneros, Prima Ballerina 73
Evelyn Cisneros, prima ballerina, Mexican American, ballet, San Francisco, audiences, theater, apprentice

It's Outta Here! 79

dribble, home plate, center field, Babe Ruth, New York Yankee, Roger Maris, Mark McGwire, St. Louis Cardinals, California, Sammy Sosa, Chicago Cubs, Dominican Republic, Spanish, foundation, donates, charity

Pancho Gonzales, Tennis Champion 85

Pancho Gonzales, Los Angeles, Mexico, energy, hyperactive, court, racket, Señor, dangerous, tournament, U.S. Singles Championship

A Japanese-American Storyteller 91

Yokohama, Japan, Allen Say, Tokyo, cartoonist's apprentice, photographer, Japanese, American

What's Your Favorite? 96

Thailand, favorites, Tom Kha Gai, broth, ginger, coconut, cilantro, Russia, matzo, chicken broth, Native American, margarine, husk, recipes

Going to the Library 103

library, telephone, entrance, Muni, passengers, turnstiles, stations, conductor, escalator, mysteries, rustled, Eric Kimmel

He Changed America by Talking 110

Dr. Martin Luther King, Jr., minister, author, sermon, presidents, Lincoln Memorial, content of their character, equal, Washington, D.C.

Kwanzaa, A New Holiday 116

Dr. Karenga, Africa, Kwanzaa, African-American celebration, kinara, symbols, principles, values

Only One, a Story About Ruby Bridges 122

Ruby Bridges, marshals, segregated, desegregated

George Washington Carver 128

fortune, fame, stuttered, George Washington Carver, Missouri, Kansas, laundry, expenses, college, agriculture, graduate, Iowa, inventor, Thomas Edison, laboratory, Tuskegee Normal School, Alabama, experimented, scientist, wizard

The Great Melting Pot 134

America, unique, immigrant, government, factories

Celebrating Diversity • EMC 795

It's fun to count.

Do you know people who count in different languages?

 My grandma is teaching me
to count in Japanese.

My auntie is teaching me
to count in Spanish.

 My uncle is teaching me
to count in Arabic.

My cousin is teaching me
to count in German.

Can you count with us?

one

(ee-chee) uno (OO-noh) (WAH-hid) eins (īns)

two

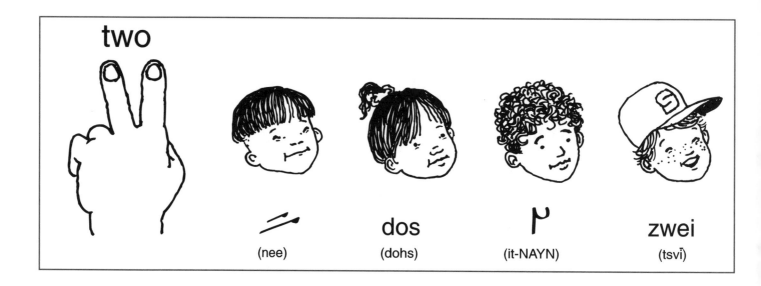

(nee) dos (dohs) (it-NAYN) zwei (tsvī)

three

(sahn) tres (trehs) (tah-LAH-tah) drei (drī)

four

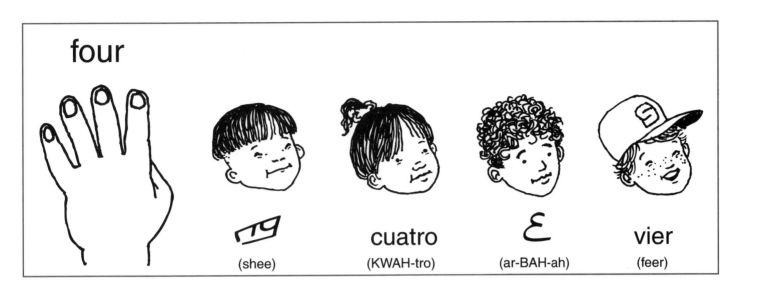

四 (shee) cuatro (KWAH-tro) ٤ (ar-BAH-ah) vier (feer)

five

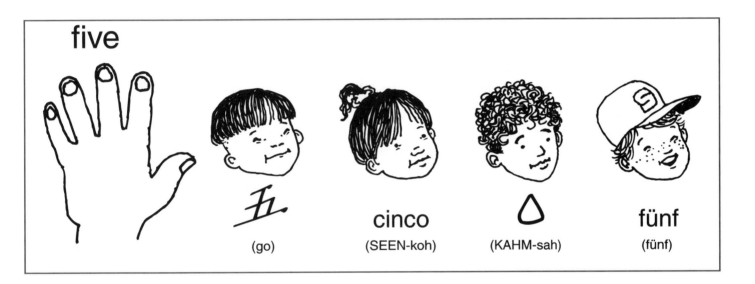

五 (go) cinco (SEEN-koh) ٥ (KAHM-sah) fünf (fünf)

one, two, three, four, five
It's fun to count!

Questions about *Count with Us*

Circle **yes** or **no**.

1. There are many different ways to count.   yes   no

2. People in the United States speak only English.   yes   no

3. Do you know someone who can count in a
   different language?   yes   no

Cut and paste to match the words with the numbers.

1	2	3	4	5
paste	paste	paste	paste	paste

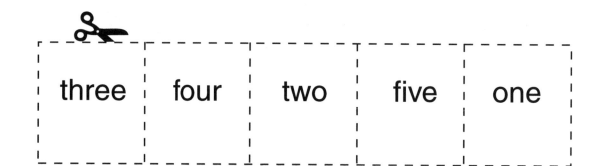

| three | four | two | five | one |

Count with Us
Reading Numbers

Read the word. Write the number.

two ☐ Draw two apples.	**four** ☐ Draw four pretzels.
one ☐ Draw one cake.	**three** ☐ Draw three cookies.

Count with Us
Put Them in Order

Cut and paste to put the numbers in order. Put the smallest number first.

paste
paste
paste
paste
paste
paste
paste
paste
paste
paste

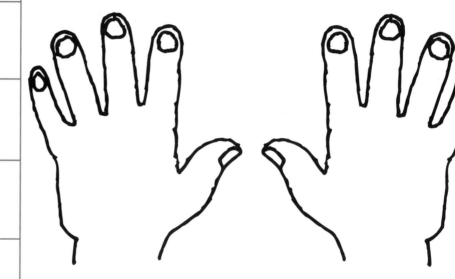

seven	four
ten	one
five	eight
two	six
three	nine

Celebrating Diversity • EMC 795

1. Write the numbers. 2. Draw a picture. 3. Cut and staple them in order.

Count with Us

A Counting Book

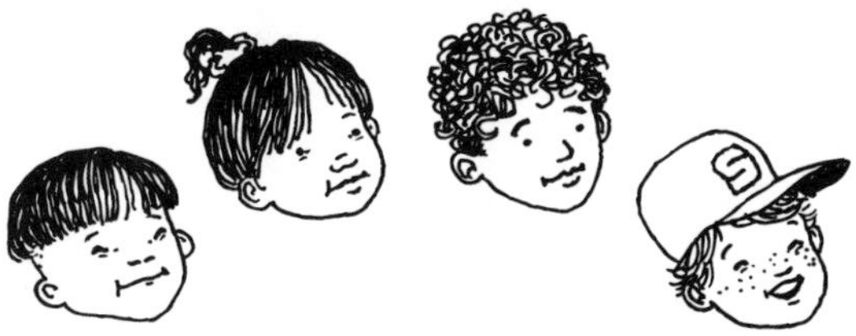

Name ______________________

one uno 一 ١ eins

two dos 二 ٢ zwei

three tres 三 ٣ drei

four cuatro 四 ٤ vier

five cinco 五 ٥ fünf

The Game

My friends and I are much the same.

We love to run and play the game.

We clap loud when a goal is made.

We cheer about how well we played.

We take our turns out in the yard.

We get the ball and kick it hard.

We stop and yell. We cheer and run.

We all believe this game is fun!

Name_____

Questions about *The Game*

1. What kind of a game is the poem about?

   a. a baseball game   c. a soccer game
   b. a football game   d. a tennis game

2. What does the poet do when a goal is made?

   a. watch the game   c. get the ball
   b. take a turn   d. clap

3. Tell three ways the two games in the poem are different.

   _____

   _____

   _____

4. Tell three ways those games are the same.

   _____

   _____

   _____

5. In the poem, does one team like soccer more than the other team? Tell why you think the way you do.

   _____

   _____

Name_____

The Game
Making New Words

Change the first letter of the underlined word to make new words that fit the next two sentences.

1. We <u>clap</u> loud when a goal is made.   **clap**

    _____ that pesky fly.   ____lap

    Lift the _____ to see what is inside.   ____lap

2. We take our turns out in the <u>yard</u>.   **yard**

    She sent me a birthday _____.   ____ard

    Mowing the lawn is _____ work.   ____ard

3. We cheer and <u>run</u>.   **run**

    The cloud covered the _____.   ____un

    Playing outside is _____.   ____un

4. My friends and I are much the <u>same</u>.   **same**

    What is your _____?   ____ame

    Slap Jack is a card _____.   ____ame

Name_____

The Game
A Game I Play

Think of a game that you play with your friends.

Write the name of the game here._____

Do you need special equipment to play?   yes   no

Do you wear a uniform when you play?   yes   no

Do others watch and cheer while you play?   yes   no

Do you think the game is played in different places?   yes   no

List all the things that you need when you play.

Draw a picture that shows you playing the game.

Name_____

The Game

Compare the Scores

Look at the scores for the two games. Then answer the questions below.

Game 1

Red Team	Blue Team
4	6

Game 2

Eagles	Hawks
3	0

1. In which game were the most goals scored?

_____

2. Which team scored the most points?

_____

3. How many more goals did the Blue Team score than the Red Team?

_____

4. How many goals were scored in all the games?

_____

The Piñata

What's a piñata?

    A clay jar

    In a star

    Hanging high

    In the sky—

        That's a piñata!

What's inside?

    Special treats,

    Yummy sweets,

    Tiny toys

    For girls and boys—

        That's what's inside!

How do you break it?

    Careful aim

    Play the game

    Swing the bat

    That is that!

        That's how you break it!

Celebrating Diversity • EMC 795

Piñatas

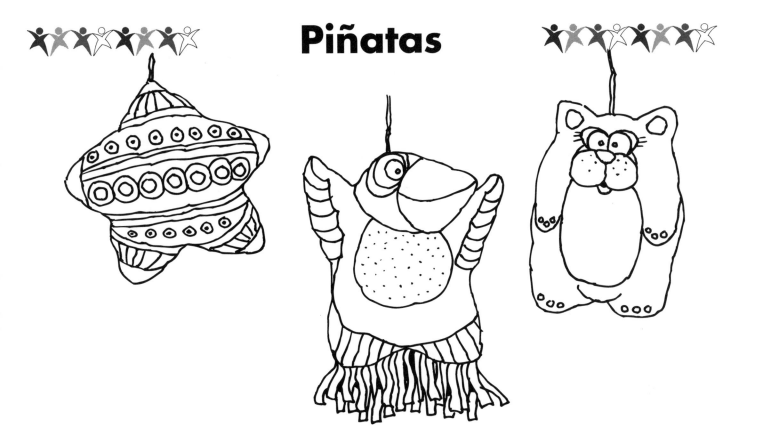

Piñatas came from Mexico. The first piñatas were animal or star shapes. They had clay pots inside. The pots were filled with yummy treats.

A piñata was hung. Children tried to hit the piñata with a stick. When the piñata broke, the treats fell to the ground.

Today piñatas are found across the United States. They are made in all shapes and sizes. Most don't have clay pots inside. It's fun to break a piñata at a picnic or a party.

Have you ever played the piñata game?

Questions about *The Piñata*

Fill in the circle beside the best answer.

1. Where did the idea of piñatas come from?

   ○ England   ○ Mexico   ○ China

2. What did the first piñatas have inside them?

   ○ clay jars filled with treats

   ○ gold and silver coins

   ○ tiny balls

3. How is the piñata broken?

   ○ It is dropped to the floor.

   ○ It is hit with a stick.

   ○ It is filled until it is too full and breaks.

4. Where are piñatas found today?

   ○ only at parties

   ○ only at picnics

   ○ at both parties and picnics

5. What would be a good treat to put in a piñata?

   ○ a red rose

   ○ an egg

   ○ a piece of candy

6. Would you like to break a piñata?

   ○ yes   ○ no

Name_____

The Piñata
Rhyming Words

Make an **X** on the pictures that rhyme with **sweet**.

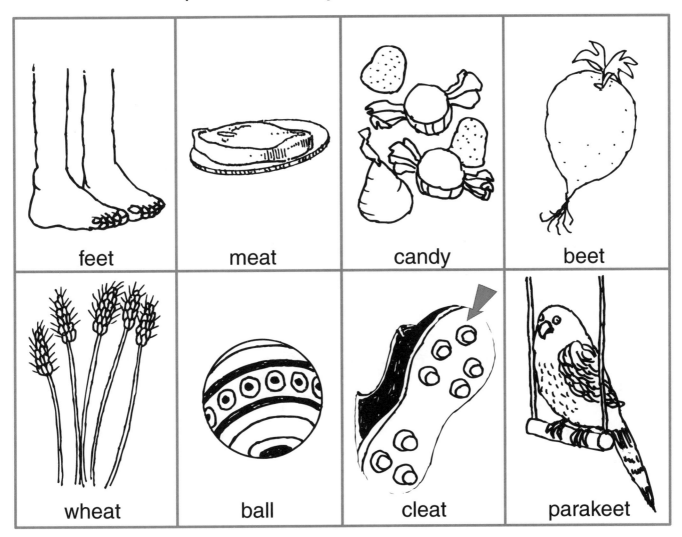

| feet | meat | candy | beet |
| wheat | ball | cleat | parakeet |

Circle the word in each sentence that rhymes with **sweet**.

1. Mom gave me a special treat.

2. Did you see Paul's neat desk?

3. The Rockets beat the Slammers by two points.

Name_____

The Piñata
Is It Breakable?

Look at the things on Pablo's shelf. Think about whether each thing is breakable. Write the name of each thing in the correct list.

Breakable   **Unbreakable**

_____   _____

_____   _____

_____   _____

_____   _____

         Celebrating Diversity • EMC 795

Name_____

Cut out the piñata. Fold on the line. Color the picture. Open the piñata. Draw at least 8 things you would like to find inside. Remember, they must not break when they fall out.

fold

✖✖✖✖✖ My Dad's Warehouse ✖✖✖✖✖

My dad works in a warehouse. The warehouse ships books to schools. The books go all over the world. Many people work in the warehouse. All the people are different. They have to work as a team to get the job done.

This is Gary.
He makes boxes to hold the books.

Rudy and Brendan are clerks. They put the right books in the right boxes.

Jean sends out catalogs. People will look in the catalogs. They will order the books they want.

This is Laura.
She puts the labels on the catalogs.

Peter checks the orders.
Bo loads them onto the truck.

My dad's team works hard.
Each member of the team is different.
Each member of the team is important.
They are happy when the job is done.

Questions about *My Dad's Warehouse*

Match the workers with their jobs.

- putting books in boxes

- making boxes

- checking orders

- putting on labels

- sending out catalogs

- loading truck

My Dad's Warehouse
Vocabulary

Cut and paste to label the pictures.

paste

paste

paste

paste

paste

paste

boxes	books	catalog
label	warehouse	truck

Name_____

My Dad's Warehouse
Ordering from a Catalog

Look at the page. Write the titles of three books you would like to order.

Evan-Moor Arts and Crafts Books

The Paper Tube Zoo $4.95
26 projects include a mouse, hippo, toucan, and squirrel. Great for finger puppets.

Folk Art Projects $7.95
The 29 projects come from other countries. Work with wood, clay, paper, and tin.

Folded Paper Projects $4.95
Learn 8 basic folds. Then use the folds to make 30 different animals.

Paper Crafts $7.95
Make decorations, hats, and masks. 31 different projects.

How to Make Greeting Cards $7.95
Create 30 special cards.

Crafts for Young Children $7.95
Try 40 projects that are fun to make.

Order Form

	Book Title	Cost
1.		
2.		
3.		
	Total	

My Dad's Warehouse
Dot-to-Dot

Connect the dots to see a machine that my dad's team uses in the warehouse. Start with 1.

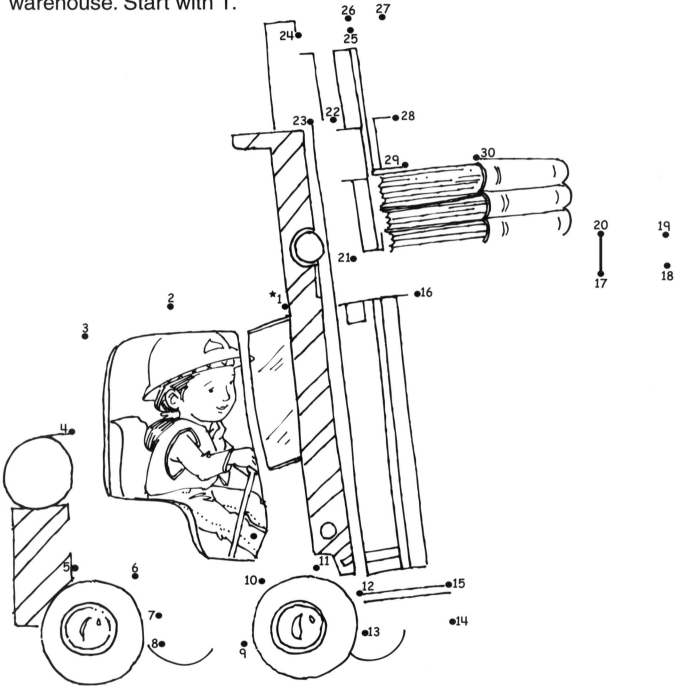

Do you know the name of this machine?   yes   no

Would you like to ride on one?   yes   no

How to Use Chopsticks

Give this a try:

1. Trap one stick between your thumb and middle finger.

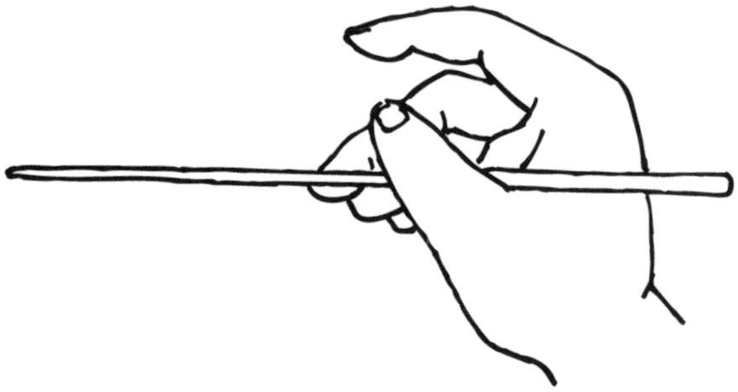

2. Put the second stick behind the tip of your thumb.

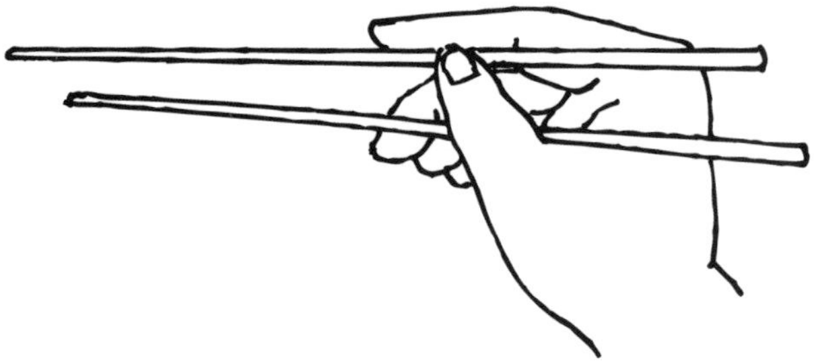

3. Wrap your pointer finger over the second stick.

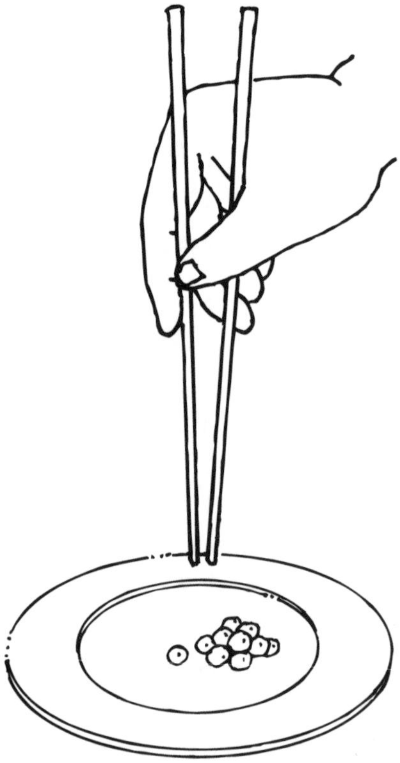

4 Tap the ends of the sticks on the plate. The ends should line up.

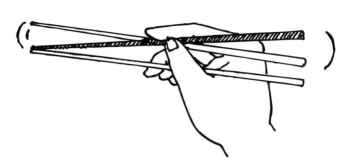

5 Move the top stick. Keep the bottom stick still.

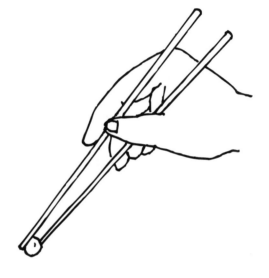

6 Pick up a piece of food between the tips.

Can you do it?

Celebrating Diversity • EMC 795

Questions about *How to Use Chopsticks*

1. How many chopsticks will you use to follow the directions?

   ○ 1   ○ 2   ○ 3   ○ 4

2. The directions tell how to use chopsticks to _____.

   ○ paint a picture   ○ play a game

   ○ pick up something

3. Many people use chopsticks to _____.

   ○ eat their food   ○ count pork chops

   ○ hold the door open

4. Have you ever used chopsticks?

   ○ yes   ○ no

Label the fingers with the correct names.

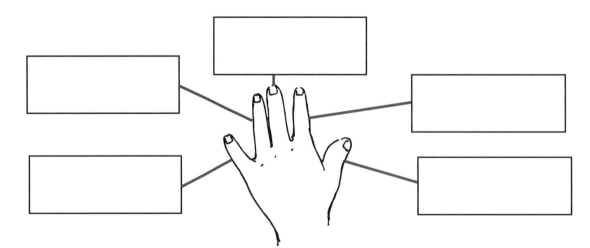

Word Box				
thumb	pointer	tall man	ring finger	pinky

How to Use Chopsticks
What Will You Use?

Write the name of the thing you will use to eat each food.

Word Box			
fork	spoon	chopsticks	fingers

_____

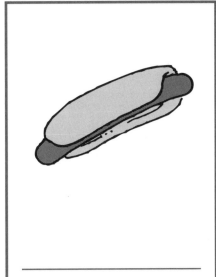

_____

_____

_____

_____

_____

Name_____

How to Use Chopsticks
Set the Table

Write the word that names each thing.

Word Box				
spoon	place mat	knife	plate	bowl
glass	chopsticks	fork	napkin	cup

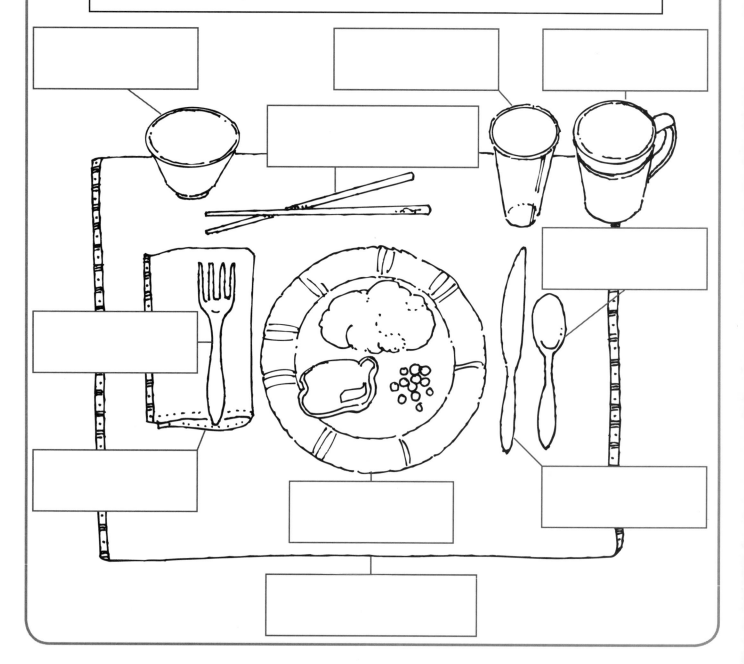

Name_____

How to Use Chopsticks
Try It Out!

Follow the directions on how to use chopsticks.
You can use chopsticks or two pencils.

Can you hold the first stick in place?   yes   no

Can you move the second stick up and down?   yes   no

Can you pick up a small wad of paper?   yes   no

Can you pick up a tiny wad of paper?   yes   no

Draw a picture to show how you felt when you tried to use chopsticks
to pick up the paper.

Hey! My name is John.
I was born on a farm in Colorado.
This is my scrapbook.
It is filled with special pictures.
Some of them are old.
Some of them are new.

Hi! My name is Nhia.
I was born on a farm in Thailand.
My family came to America.
This is my story cloth.
My grandmother made it.
She stitched a story of our family.
You can see pictures.

Each person has a way to remember things.
John and Nhia have two different ways of remembering.

Would you like to learn about my family?

I like this picture of my house. It was built over 100 years ago. That's my great-great-grandpa.

Here is my great-grandpa. He lived and worked on the farm when he was a boy.

Here is my great-grandma with her horse. She grew up on a farm, too.

Looking at my scrapbook is a good way of remembering. It helps me see how some things are the same and how some things are different.

I like to look at the story cloth.
I can feel the stitches.

See my great-grandfather and his brothers. They are leaving China.

Here is the house where my mother lived as a child. It was made of wood and bamboo. It had a palm-leaf roof.

This plane brought my father and mother to the United States.

Looking at the story cloth is a good way of remembering. It reminds me of happy times and sad times. It helps me remember my family's long journey.

Celebrating Diversity • EMC 795

Questions about *Two Ways to Remember*

1. What does John use to help him remember?

_____

2. What does Nhia use to help her remember?

_____

3. How are the two things alike?

_____

4. How are they different?

_____

_____

5. What do you use to help you remember?

_____

_____

_____

_____

Name_____

Two Ways to Remember
Vocabulary

Match the words with the phrase that tells what they mean.

tractor   ● a long trip

memories   ● a giant grass with hollow stems

stitched   ● sewed with thread

bamboo   ● things that are remembered

journey   ● a vehicle used to pull equipment

Use one of the words from the list above to complete each sentence.

1. I talk with my grandmother about her _____ of
   the past.

2. Have you ever ridden on a _____?

3. To celebrate the baby's birth, she _____ a quilt.

4. My father took a _____ to see the place where
   he was born.

5. Some houses in Thailand are made of _____.

Name_____

Two Ways to Remember
Asking Questions

One way to make memories is to ask questions and remember the answers. Choose another student, a member of your family, or a teacher. Ask the questions below. Write down the answers.

Where was the first school you went to?

_____

_____

What thing in the school was your favorite thing?

_____

_____

What book in the school was your favorite book?

_____

What do you remember about your first day of school?

_____

_____

What was the most important thing you learned?

_____

_____

_____

Name_____

Two Ways to Remember
Journeys

Circle **yes** or **no**.

Has your family ever moved to a new place?   yes   no

Did you go on the journey?   yes   no

Was the journey taken before you were born?   yes   no

Fill in the circles below to tell about the journey.

1. My family took a journey...

   ○ a long time ago   ○ after I was born

2. My family moved to...

   ○ a new house   ○ a new town   ○ a new country

3. The move made my family...

   ○ happy   ○ unhappy

4. When I grow up I would like to...

   ○ take a journey of my own   ○ stay where I am today

Write a sentence to tell why.

_____

_____

_____

✿✿✿✿✿✿ My Granny's Bread ✿✿✿✿✿✿

My granny makes a special bread. It doesn't look like the bread you buy at the store. It looks like a flat pancake. It's made from potatoes. The recipe came from Norway with Granny's parents. The bread is called lefse.

When Granny was a little girl, she helped her mother make the bread. Her mother mixed the dough. She added coal to the cook stove to make it hot. She took a piece of the dough and rolled it flat. She spread the big, round circle of dough on the top of the stove. Granny's job was to turn the bread when one side was cooked. Granny slid a long, thin stick under the bread. She flipped it over.

Celebrating Diversity • EMC 795

Now I watch Granny make her bread. She lets me use the rolling pin to flatten the dough. Granny uses a special rolling pin. The rolling pin has bumps on it. It makes bumpy, flat dough. The bumps help the bread cook.

Granny doesn't have a coal stove anymore. She cooks the bread on a big, flat pan called a griddle. This is what Granny does:

She boils the potatoes.

She mashes them.

She adds butter, cream, and salt.

She mixes in flour.

Then Granny rolls the dough. I watch the bread cook. I turn the bread with a spatula. I wrap the cooked bread in a towel. It will stay warm while Granny and I work.

Finally it is time to eat. My dad wraps his bread around a sausage. Granny likes hers with lutefisk. (Lutefisk is cod that has been soaked in lye.) I put brown sugar and butter on mine. I roll it up. I bite off a yummy corner. Ummmmmmm— lefse!

Name_____

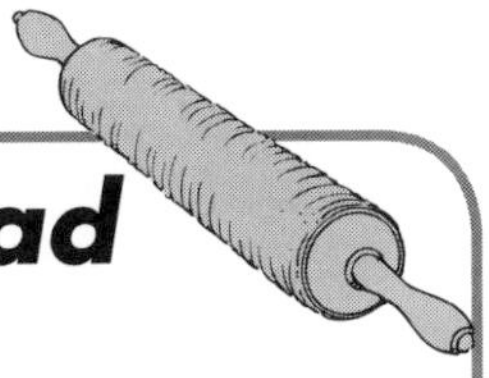

Questions about *My Granny's Bread*

1. What is lefse?

_____

2. Complete the table below to show that you understand the story.

	Granny's Lefse	A Loaf of Bread
Main ingredient		
What does it look like?		
How do you eat it?		

3. What is special about Granny's rolling pin?

_____

4. Many families make special breads. Tell about the bread your family likes the best. How is it like lefse? How is it different?

_____

_____

_____

My Granny's Bread
Vocabulary

This story uses two Norwegian words. Match each word with the phrase that gives its English meaning.

lefse   ● codfish soaked in lye

lutefisk   ● flat rounds of potato bread

Choose a word from the Word Box to complete the sentences below.

Word Box					
rolls	dough	griddle	sausage	coal	spatula

1. Granny mixes potatoes, cream, butter, salt, and flour to make

   her _____.

2. Granny _____ the dough to flatten it.

3. When she was a little girl, Granny added _____
   to the stove to make it hot.

4. _____ is a breakfast meat.

5. A _____ is used to turn pancakes.

6. A flat pan for cooking is called a _____.

My Granny's Bread
Putting Steps in Order

Cut and paste to put the steps for making lefse in order.

1	**paste**
2	**paste**
3	**paste**
4	**paste**
5	**paste**
6	**paste**

Mash the potatoes.

Add butter, cream, salt, and flour.

Boil the potatoes.

Enjoy the yummy bread.

Roll the dough.

Cook the bread.

Name_____

My Granny's Bread
Eating Bread

Lefses are rolled up and eaten.

Think of the different ways that you eat bread.
List as many as you can.

_____   _____

_____   _____

_____   _____

_____   _____

What is your favorite way to eat bread?
Draw a picture and write about it here.

_____

_____

_____

_____

_____

Jim Abbott

Baseball Pitcher

"You can do anything if you are determined and work hard." The words marched in Jim's head. He wanted to be a pitcher for a major-league baseball team. He worked hard. He practiced throwing. He practiced catching. He played baseball every chance he had.

When he was eleven, he joined a Little League team. The team needed a pitcher. Jim said, "I'll do it." He took the mound. He pitched a no-hitter!

Jim kept working hard. He was determined. He pitched for his high school team. He got better. He went to college. He pitched for his college team. He got better. He was chosen to be the starting pitcher for Team U.S.A. in the Pan-American Games. He got better. He pitched for the U.S. Olympics baseball team. They won a gold medal!

In April 1989, Jim Abbott's dream came true. He became a pitcher for the California Angels. He earned twelve wins that year. That was more than any other major-league rookie. Jim was a big-league pitcher!

Why is Jim Abbott's story so special? Jim set a goal and worked hard to reach it. He didn't let anything stop him. He was born without a right hand.

Many people see Jim as handicapped. They feel sorry for him. Jim does not consider himself handicapped. He does not want people to feel sorry for him. He does not want to be known as a one-handed man who can pitch. He is a pitcher who just happens to have only one hand.

Celebrating Diversity • EMC 795

Name_____

Questions about *Jim Abbott*

1. What did Jim Abbott want to do?

_____

_____

2. What did Jim Abbott do to make his dream come true?

_____

_____

3. What special challenge did Jim Abbott overcome?

_____

_____

4. What lesson can people learn from Jim Abbott?

_____

_____

_____

_____

Name_____

Jim Abbott
Baseball Words

Match these baseball words with their correct meaning.

pitch   • a first-year player

starting pitcher   • to throw the ball for a batter to hit

rookie   • a game where no batter gets a hit

no-hitter   • the player who is pitching at the
                                           beginning of a game

---

Choose one of the words above to complete each sentence.

1. Jim Abbott was the _____ for Team U.S.A.

2. The first time Jim Abbott pitched, he threw a _____.

3. When he was a _____, Jim Abbott had a better win
   record than any other first-year player.

4. Some people are surprised that Jim Abbott can _____.

5. When you try something for the first time you are

   a _____.

Name_____

Cut and paste to put the things that Jim Abbott did in the correct order.

1	**paste**
2	**paste**
3	**paste**
4	**paste**
5	**paste**
6	**paste**

Jim won an Olympic gold medal.

Jim joined a Little League team.

Jim pitched for his college team.

Jim decided to be a pitcher.

Jim pitched for the California Angels.

Jim pitched for his high school team.

Jim Abbott

Determination and Hard Work

Jim Abbott believes that you can do anything if you are determined and work hard. Think about something you really want to do. Write it here.

My Goal:

I want to _____.

Think about the things you will need to do to reach your goal. Write them here.

In order to reach my goal I will have to:

_____

_____

_____

_____

_____

_____

How does rice grow?

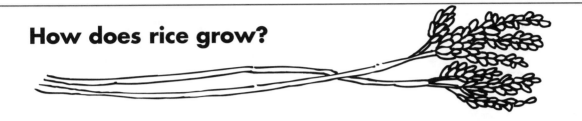

It's planted in big fields called rice paddies. The paddies are flooded with water. When rice plants are young, they're bright green. They turn golden brown when they're ready to harvest. The tips of the plants hold the kernels of rice that we eat.

Rice for breakfast.

Rice for lunch.

Rice for dinner.

Sam's family eats rice at every meal.

How does corn grow?

It's planted in rows in big fields. The fields are irrigated. Farmers make little ditches between the rows. They pump water into the ditches to water each corn plant. Kernels of corn come from the ears that grow on the stalks. The stalks, the ears, and the leaves are chopped up to feed animals.

Oscar's family eats corn flakes for breakfast.
Sylvie takes corn chips in her lunch bag for lunch.
Do you like corn on the cob?

How does wheat grow?

It's planted in big fields. Sometimes farmers irrigate their wheat crops. Sometimes they let the rain water their crops. Grains of wheat grow in a head. The head is at the end of a thin stalk. The green wheat sways in the breeze. When the wheat is ripe, it turns golden brown.

Celine and her family eat wheat all through the day.

Name_____

Questions about *How Does It Grow?*

1. Which three things did the story explain?

   ○ rice, corn, wheat

   ○ rice, beans, corn

   ○ corn, oats, peanuts

2. What part of the rice plant contains the kernels that we eat?

   ○ base of the roots

   ○ next to the leaves

   ○ tip of the plant

3. What color is rice when its ready to harvest?

   ○ light green   ○ golden brown   ○ deep orange

4. Where do the grains of wheat grow?

   ○ on the head   ○ on the ear   ○ on the stalk

5. Where do the kernels of corn grow?

   ○ on the head   ○ on the ear   ○ on the stalk

6. What part of the corn is used to feed livestock?

   ○ only the kernels

   ○ only the leaves

   ○ the stalks, the leaves, and the ears

Name_____

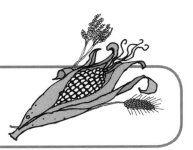

Cut and paste to label the parts of the plants.

Corn

Wheat

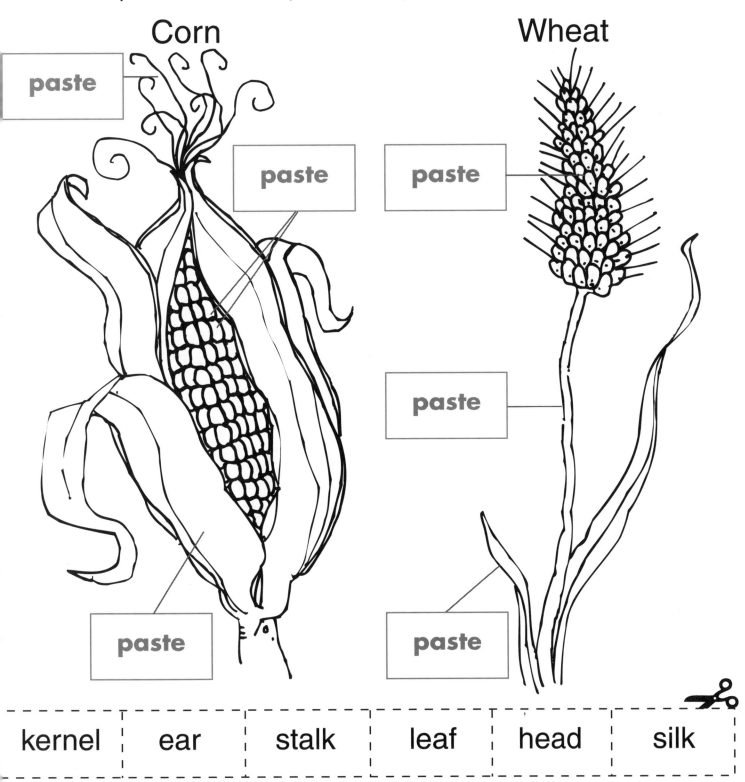

paste

paste

paste

paste

paste

paste

kernel	ear	stalk	leaf	head	silk

Name_____

How Does It Grow?

Do You Eat It?

Do you eat rice?   yes   no

Circle the pictures that show ways you eat rice.

 Cereal    Rice Burrito    Steamed Rice    Fried Rice

 Rice Pudding

Rice Crackers

Do you eat corn?   yes   no

Circle the pictures that show ways you eat corn.

Corn Chowder   Corn on the Cob   Popcorn

 Cornflakes

Corn Chips

Corn Bread

Do you eat wheat?   yes   no

Circle the pictures that show ways you eat wheat.

 Crackers   Wheat Berries   Shredded Wheat Cereal

Bread    Bulgur Wheat

Name_____

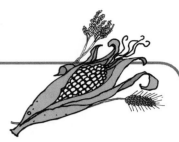

How Does It Grow?
Irrigation

Some farmers **irrigate** their crops. That means they supply the crops with water.

1. How do farmers irrigate rice fields?

_____

_____

2. How do farmers irrigate cornfields?

_____

_____

3. How do farmers irrigate wheat fields?

_____

_____

4. Do you water your garden?   yes   no

   Do you water houseplants?   yes   no

   Do you irrigate anything else? _____

_____

Susan Butcher

A Champion

Have you ever been in a race? There is a special race that takes place in Alaska every year. The race starts in Anchorage. It ends in Nome. This famous race is called the Iditarod.

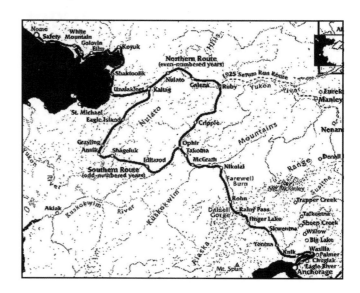

To get to the finish line, Iditarod racers and their sled dog teams cross two mountain ranges. They ford ice-covered rivers. They slide over the frozen Bering Sea. The temperature is very cold. It might be ⁻50°F (⁻45°C). The winds are very strong. They might be over 140 miles (225 km) per hour.

Becoming an Iditarod Champion

Susan Butcher was born in Massachusetts. She always loved animals. She bought her first husky (or sled dog) when she was fifteen. A year later she bought another husky. Susan's mother said that their house was not big enough for the two dogs. Susan moved to Maine to live with her grandmother.

In 1975 Susan moved to Fairbanks, Alaska. She lived in a remote cabin. The only way to get to the cabin was by plane. Susan chopped her own firewood. She hunted for the meat she ate. She hauled her water from a nearby creek. She took care of her huskies.

Susan heard about the Iditarod. She wanted to race in it. She needed a sled and more dogs. Each musher (that's what racers in the Iditarod are called) takes from seven to  fourteen dogs on the race. Mushers also carry snowshoes, sleeping bags, boots for the dogs' feet, and food for the dogs and themselves.

In 1978 Susan took part in her first Iditarod. She was hooked. She enters every year. She has won the race four times. She is one of only two racers ever to do that.

A Solitary Life

Susan lives a very different life than someone who lives in a busy city. She doesn't have a television. She doesn't use a clock or a calendar. For months in the winter, her husband is the only person she sees.

When she is not racing, Susan and her husband take care of their 150 dogs. Susan trains the dogs. She takes them on walks and runs with them every day. She teaches them to pull together in a team.

Questions about *Susan Butcher*

1. What is the Iditarod?

   ○ a tall flagpole

   ○ a town in Alaska

   ○ a race

2. Where is the Iditarod held?

   ○ in Alabama

   ○ in Alaska

   ○ in Massachusetts

3. To be in the Iditarod you must have...

   ○ a sled   ○ seven to fourteen sled dogs

   ○ snowshoes   ○ all of the above

4. Susan Butcher lives

   ○ in a busy city

   ○ in a quiet town

   ○ in a remote cabin

5. An Iditarod racer is called a

   ○ musher   ○ husky   ○ runner

6. A good motto for Susan Butcher would be…

   ○ Rely on your friends to get you through.

   ○ Be independent and work hard.

   ○ Don't do more than you have to.

Name_____

Susan Butcher
Vocabulary

Draw a line from the word to the part of the picture that shows its meaning.

sled dog

dog sled

snowshoe

musher

Match the first part of the sentence with the correct ending.

Iditarod racers cross   • together in a team.

The dogs ford   • her own firewood.

The dogs must pull   • two mountain ranges.

Susan Butcher chops   • ice-covered rivers.

Name_____

Susan Butcher
Compound Words

Write the two words that make up each of these compound words.

firewood   _____   _____

grandmother   _____   _____

someone   _____   _____

nearby   _____   _____

Susan lived in **Fairbanks**, Alaska.

What two words make up the name of the town where Susan lived?

_____   _____

Think about the meaning of the two words.

What do the words tell you about the town?

_____

_____

Think of the town where you live.

Give the town a new compound word name.

_____   _____

Why did you choose the words you did?

_____

Name_____

Susan Butcher

Compare Your Life with Susan Butcher's Life

Fill in the boxes to complete the chart.

	Susan Butcher	Me
Place We Live • location • weather		
Things We Use • television • clock • calendar		
Things We Do • walk dogs • visit with friends • go to the store		

Write to tell how your life differs from Susan Butcher's life.

_____

_____

_____

Running to Fame

Jesse Owens was born on a farm in Alabama. His parents were sharecroppers. Jesse was skinny. He was often sick. But he loved to run. Jesse's parents wanted a better life. So when Jesse was nine, the family moved to Ohio.

In Ohio Jessie met a man who would change his life. The man was Charles Riley, a teacher and coach. Coach Riley taught Jesse to run and jump. Jesse worked hard. Jesse was an important member of his junior high track team. He began to set records.

Jesse kept running. He ran on a team while he went to high school. He ran on a team while he went to college. He set many more records.

In 1936 the Olympics were held in Berlin. Jesse Owens was on the United States' team. He won four gold medals. He set world records in three events.

Jesse Owens became a great track-and-field runner. People all over the world knew Jesse Owens and watched him run. They thought he was a hero.

Jesse Owens began life as a poor, sickly boy. He learned how to run. He ran so fast that he became famous all over the world.

Questions about *Running to Fame*

Choose the best answer.

1. Jesse Owens was a famous

   ○ farmer   ○ runner   ○ teacher

2. Jesse's parents moved to Ohio because

   ○ they didn't like cold weather

   ○ they wanted to live near a lake

   ○ they wanted a better life

3. In this story, what person changed Jesse's life?

   ○ his father   ○ his track coach   ○ his brother

4. What do you think made Jesse a good runner?

   ○ fast shoes   ○ hard work   ○ vitamins

5. **Setting a record** means

   ○ running faster than anyone else has run

   ○ turning on the music

   ○ putting the plates and spoons on a table

6. Jesse ran on many different teams. Mark all the ones that are in this story.

   ○ junior high track team   ○ U.S. Olympic team

   ○ high school track team   ○ Roadrunners' track team

   ○ Alabama track team   ○ college track team

Jesse

Running to Fame
Words About Running

Jesse Owens was a very fast runner. Write **slow** or **fast** by each phrase below.

1. swift as an arrow _____

2. at a snail's pace _____

3. plodding along _____

4. fleet as the wind _____

5. like a blue streak _____

6. behind schedule _____

7. like wildfire _____

8. like molasses in January _____

9. like greased lightning _____

Use one of the "fast" phrases above to complete each of these sentences.

The jet soared through the sky _____.

The horse galloped _____.

The water in the river rushed by _____.

Name_____

Running to Fame
Keys to Success

Jesse Owens was a great runner. He had a good coach and he worked hard. Coaching and hard work were keys to his success.

Think of two things that you do well. Write one in each box. Then label each key with one of the keys to your success.

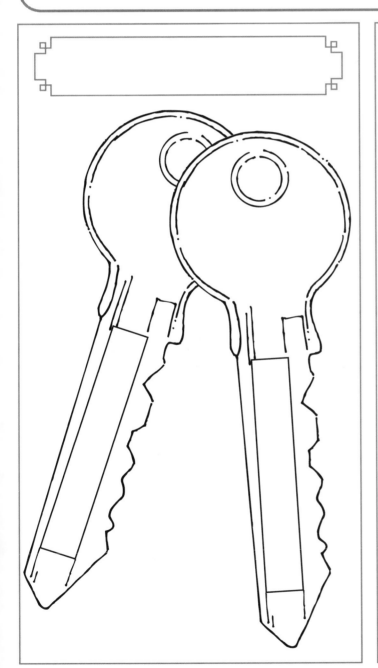

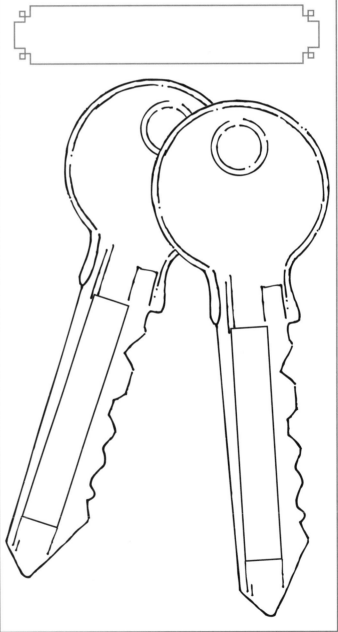

Jesse

Running to Fame
Special Compound Words

Sharecroppers farm land that they don't own. They prepare the earth. They plant the seeds. They take care of the crops. When the crops are harvested, sharecroppers keep part of the crop. They give the rest to the owner of the land. It is like paying rent for the land.

The name **sharecropper** comes from the two words **share** and **crop**. These farmers share their crops.

Look at the compound words below that name other jobs. Write the two words that make up each compound word.

dishwasher

	+	

cheerleader

	+	

shipbuilder

	+	

clockmaker

	+	

 # Evelyn Cisneros
Prima Ballerina

On the first day of school everyone stared at me. The other kids laughed and pointed. They teased me because I looked different. I was the only Mexican American in the whole school. I was afraid to raise my hand in class. I never talked to anyone. I was very unhappy.

My mother wanted to help. She took me to ballet class. In class no one pointed or laughed. I loved turning and leaping. At first I went to ballet once a week. Soon I was going every day. I helped to teach the new dancers. I performed in front of audiences.

Celebrating Diversity • EMC 795

When I was fourteen I went to school from 7:30 a.m. to 2:30 p.m. Then I went to ballet. I practiced until dinnertime. After dinner I performed at a ballet theater.

When I was sixteen I became an apprentice with the San Francisco Ballet School. I moved to San Francisco and became a real ballerina.

I still practice and study every day. I have traveled all over the world. I have met many people and danced for them. Who would have guessed that the shy little brown girl would become a prima ballerina?

I remember the girl I was in kindergarten. I remember crying because I was different from the others. What if my mother hadn't taken me to ballet class?

Sometimes I worry about other shy boys and girls. I want to tell them that being different isn't bad. I want to tell them how hard work made my dream come true. I want to dance for them.

Name_____

Questions about *Evelyn Cisneros*

1. Why was Evelyn unhappy at school?

_____

_____

2. How did Evelyn's mother help her?

_____

_____

3. Do you think fourteen-year-old Evelyn's school day was like most students' days? Tell why you think as you do.

_____

_____

_____

4. What does Evelyn want to tell shy boys and girls?

_____

_____

_____

Name_____

Evelyn Cisneros
Vocabulary

Ballet is a special kind of dancing.

A woman who dances in a ballet is called a **ballerina**.

All the dancers who work together are called a **company**.

The main dancer in a company is called a **prima ballerina**.

A. Use the dance words above to complete these sentences.

1. Evelyn wanted to be a _____.

2. She took _____ lessons.

3. When she was sixteen she joined the San Francisco

   Ballet _____.

4. She worked and practiced hard. She became the

   _____.

B. Answer these questions about ballet.

1. Have you ever been to ballet class?   yes   no

2. Do you like to turn and leap?   yes   no

3. Do you like to perform for an audience?   yes   no

Evelyn Cisneros
Being an Apprentice

An **apprentice** is a special kind of student.
An apprentice studies with a master.

A **master** is someone who is very good at something.
The apprentice tries to learn how to be like the master.

Cut and paste to show which words describe the apprentice and which words describe the master.

Apprentice

paste

paste

paste

Master

paste

paste

paste

teacher

learner

beginner

a person with great skill

needs to learn how

ready to share talent

Name_____

Evelyn Cisneros
Sharing a Talent

Evelyn Cisneros was shy, but she loved performing ballet for others. She learned a skill that she wanted to share with others.

Think of something that you love to do.

• Are you really good at it?

• How could you share that thing with others?

• Would sharing your special skill make you feel good about yourself?

Fill in the chart below.

My Special Skill:	
What makes me good:	
How I can get better:	
How I can share it:	
How sharing it will help me:	

It's Outta Here!

It's a great feeling to swing the bat and slam the ball. You know as you hit it if the hit was solid or not. You know if the ball will only dribble in front of home plate. You know whether it has a chance to sail over the fence in center field. "It's outta here!"

When you hit a home run, it's a good feeling. Your teammates cheer. You hold your head high as you circle the bases.

The famous baseball player Babe Ruth was a good home run hitter. He was a New York Yankee. During the time Babe Ruth played baseball, he hit 714 home runs. In 1927 he hit 60 home runs. No one else hit more home runs in a single season until 1961. In 1961 Roger Maris hit 61 home runs.

Then came the summer of 1998. Two great home run hitters played baseball. Both men hit the ball hard. Both men broke the record. Both men were happy to have been part of a great home run race.

Mark McGwire plays for the St. Louis Cardinals. He was born in California. He has light hair and light eyes. He has one son named Matthew. Mark speaks English. He played ball in college before he played in the major leagues.

Sammy Sosa plays for the Chicago Cubs. He was born in the Dominican Republic. He has dark hair and dark eyes. He signed his first major league contract when he was only sixteen. He has three children. Sammy speaks Spanish and English.

Both Mark and Sammy believe it is important to work hard. They work hard at hitting home runs. But they work hard at helping others, too. Sammy donated 40 computers to schools in the Dominican Republic for every home run that he hit in 1998. The Sammy Sosa Foundation supports children in the United States and the Dominican Republic. Mark donates over $1 million each year to charity.

Mark McGwire and Sammy Sosa are heroes on the baseball field. They are different men with different ideas. But they both believe in helping others. They are home run heroes with heart.

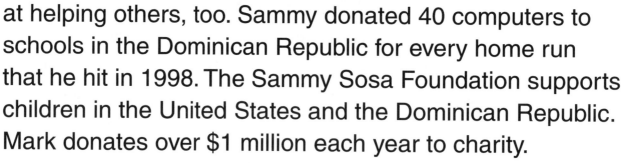

Name_____

Questions about *It's Outta Here!*

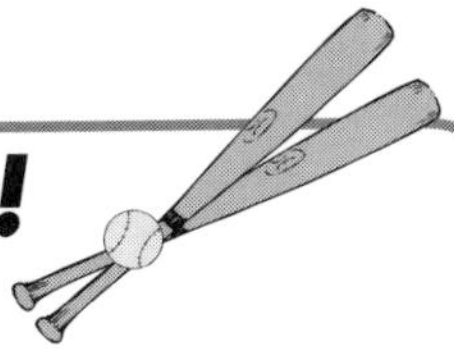

1. What does **It's outta here!** mean?

   _____

   _____

2. Name four good home run hitters.

   _____   _____

   _____   _____

3. What is the same about Sammy Sosa and Mark McGwire?

   _____

   _____

   _____

4. What is different about Sammy Sosa and Mark McGwire?

   _____

   _____

5. What does the phrase **home run heroes with heart** mean?

   _____

   _____

It's Outta Here!
Baseball Words

Some words have special meanings when they refer to baseball. Circle the sentences that use the baseball meaning.

home run

Jeff hit a home run.

Jeff had to run home for the book.

swing

Mary loves to swing at recess.

Swing the bat over the plate.

bat

The bat hunts at night.

Try to hit the ball with the bat.

home plate

When you cross home plate you score a run.

Grandma took the plate home.

center field

The middle of the outfield is called center field.

The farmer drove the tractor into the center of his field.

circle the bases

The runner will circle the bases to score a run.

Circle the bases in the picture.

Name_____

It's Outta Here!

Helping Others

Sammy Sosa and Mark McGwire think that it is important to help other people.

1. What is one thing that Sammy Sosa did to help others?

_____

_____

2. What is one thing that Mark McGwire did to help others?

_____

_____

3. What is something that you have done to help others?

_____

_____

4. What would you like to do to help others when you grow up?

_____

_____

_____

Name_____

It's Outta Here!
How Far Will It Have to Go?

Look at the picture of the ball field.
Answer the questions about home runs.

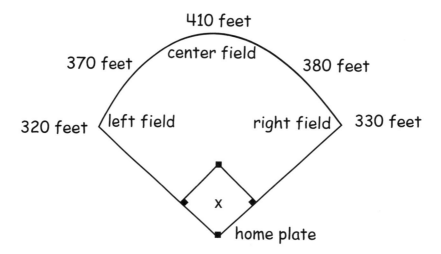

410 feet

center field

370 feet

380 feet

320 feet

left field

right field

330 feet

x

home plate

1. How far does the ball have to be hit to go over the fence in center field?

_____

2. How far does the ball have to be hit to go over the fence in right field?

_____

3. How far does the ball have to be hit to go over the fence in left field?

_____

4. Sammy hit the ball 450 feet into left field. Did he hit a home run?

_____

Pancho Gonzales
Tennis Champion

Pancho Gonzales grew up in Los Angeles. His parents had been born in Mexico. Pancho was a busy child. He couldn't sit still. He had so much energy he was always moving. He was often in trouble. Today teachers and doctors might call him hyperactive.

Pancho asked his mother for a bike. His mother thought bikes were too dangerous. She bought Pancho a tennis racket instead. No one in Pancho's family had ever played tennis.

Pancho took the racket to a tennis court. He started to hit an old ball he found on the ground. He loved it! He watched and practiced. He never let his racket out of his sight. He even slept with it. Sometimes he talked to it!

"Good morning, Señor Tennis Racket."

"Good morning, Señor Gonzales."

Pancho never had real tennis lessons. But he worked hard at learning to play. He hit the ball hard. He moved fast. He won a tennis tournament when he was eleven. He got better and better.

In 1945 Pancho stopped playing tennis and served in the U.S. Navy. Then Pancho began playing tennis again. In 1949 he won the U.S. Singles Championship. In 1950 Pancho won the title again. Pancho kept playing tennis. He won many more championships.

Pancho continued to play tennis until he died in 1995. He spent most of his time teaching others the game that made such a difference in his life.

 Celebrating Diversity • EMC 795

Name_____

Questions about *Pancho Gonzales*

1. What was Pancho's problem when he was a child?

_____

_____

2. Was playing tennis a family activity in the Gonzales family?
   Explain how you know.

_____

_____

3. What did Pancho do to become a champion tennis player?

_____

_____

4. Was Pancho's first tennis racket important to him?
   Explain how you know.

_____

_____

_____

Pancho Gonzales
Understanding Tennis Words

court—Tennis is played on a tennis **court**.

net—There is a **net** in the center of the tennis court.

racket—A player hits the tennis ball with a **racket**.

Read the pairs of sentences below. Circle the words **court**, **net**, and **racket** in the sentences. Tell whether each word uses its tennis meaning.

1. The two boys met at the tennis court each morning.

     tennis   not tennis

 The judge called the court to order.

     tennis   not tennis

2. The fisherman threw his net into the water.

     tennis   not tennis

 The girl hit the ball over the net.

     tennis   not tennis

3. The chickens made such a racket that I couldn't sleep.

     tennis   not tennis

 I hit the ball with my racket.

     tennis   not tennis

Name_____

Pancho Gonzales
Funny Names

In the story, Pancho talked to his tennis racket as if it were human. He called it **"Señor Tennis Racket."** Match the sports equipment with the correct names.

Fearless Fabian Football

Mighty Max Mallet

Pretty Peggy Paddle

Baby Bouncy Ball

Think of a name for a baseball bat. Make sure that the name has three parts and each part starts with the same beginning sound.

_____

_____

Do you have a stuffed animal or a toy that you talk to?   yes   no

Name_____

Pancho Gonzales
Working Hard To Be the Best

Pancho Gonzales worked hard to become a champion.

Think of a sport you would like to do well. Write it here.

```
┌─────────────────────────────────────────────────┐
│                                                   │
│                                                   │
│                                                   │
│                                                   │
└─────────────────────────────────────────────────┘
```

What will you have to practice?

_____   _____

_____   _____

_____   _____

Draw a picture to show what you will look like after your hard work.

A Japanese-American Storyteller

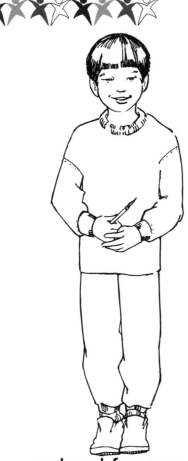

Once upon a time there was a boy named Allen. He was born in Yokohama, Japan. When he was six years old, he wanted to draw cartoons. When he was twelve, he was sent to live with his grandmother in Tokyo. He didn't get along with her. He moved into an apartment of his own. He became a cartoonist's apprentice. He drew and painted and helped his teacher.

When Allen was sixteen, his father decided to go to the United States. He took Allen with him. Allen went to school for one year. Then he went to work. He went from job to job. He tried many schools. He wrote a book about his life in Japan. He became a photographer.

Years passed and Allen Say wrote many more books. He wrote about parts of his life. He helped his readers understand life in Japan and life in America. Many of his books have won awards.

Allen Say is Japanese. Allen Say is American. Allen Say is a good storyteller. He tells stories with his brush and ink and words.

Name_____

Questions about
A Japanese-American Storyteller

1. When did Allen Say decide that he wanted to draw cartoons?

   _____

   _____

2. Why was it unusual for Allen Say to have his own apartment in Tokyo?

   _____

   _____

3. When did Allen Say come to America?

   _____

   _____

4. Which sentence best describes Allen Say?

   ○ He only sees things one way.

   ○ He is afraid to try new things.

   ○ He is a bridge between two different countries.

5. Have you ever read a book written by Allen Say?   yes   no

   Write the name of the book here. _____

   _____

Name_____

A Japanese-American Storyteller
Vocabulary

Draw a line from the word to the sentence that tells what
it means.

cartoonist   ● a rented room or rooms

apprentice   ● someone who uses words to tell a story

apartment   ● someone who uses pictures to tell a story

storyteller   ● a student learning a skill from a master

What would you like to do when you grow up?

_____

_____

Have you ever lived in an apartment?   yes   no

Allen Say lived alone. Who do you live with?

_____

_____

A Japanese-American Storyteller
Drawing a Cartoon

A **cartoonist** tells a story with a series of drawings. Draw four pictures to show something funny that happened to you.

Name_____

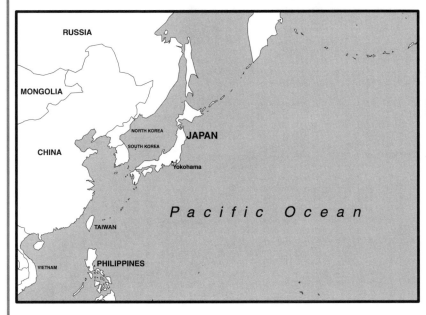

Find Japan on the map.

Draw a red circle around it.

Find California on the map.

Draw a blue circle
around it.

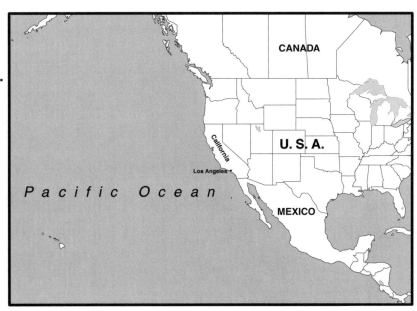

What ocean is between Yokohama and Los Angeles?

_____

✶✶✶✶✶What's Your Favorite?✶✶✶✶✶

My mother was born in Thailand.
We have rice with every meal.
My favorite recipe is Tom Kha Gai.

Tom Kha Gai

1. Mix and cook:
   chicken broth
   lime juice
   chopped ginger
   sugar
   coconut milk
2. Add diced, cooked chicken.
3. Spoon over rice.
4. Top with cilantro leaves and crushed red pepper.

Would you like a bite?

My grandmother was born in Russia.

She makes matzo ball soup for me.

I get to help make the matzo balls.

We put the cooked balls in a bowl.

Then we pour chicken broth over them.

Matzo Balls

1. Beat the egg whites.

2. Fold in the yolks and the matzo meal.

3. Roll the mixture into small balls.

4. Chill the balls for at least one hour.

5. Put the balls in boiling water.
   Cover the pan. Cook until fluffy.

Eat! It's good for you!

My aunt is a Native American.
When we visit her, she always roasts
corn for me. It's my favorite food.

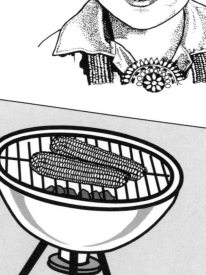

Roasted Corn

What You Need:
sweet corn
butter or margarine
salt

What You Do:
1. Soak the ears of corn, husk and all, in water for at least 15 minutes.
2. Set them on a grill. Turn them every few minutes. Cook for about 12 minutes.
3. Take them off the grill. Peel the husk and silk. Butter the corn. Sprinkle with salt.

We each have different favorites. Sometimes our favorites come from special family recipes. Sometimes our favorites come from places we have lived or visited.

It's fun to try new foods. Sometimes that's a good way to find new favorites.

Questions about *What's Your Favorite?*

1. When might you eat Tom Kha Gai?

   ○ for a snack   ○ for supper   ○ for breakfast

2. When might you eat matzo ball soup?

   ○ when you're sick   ○ when you're hot   ○ when you're camping

3. When might you eat roasted corn?

   ○ at a movie   ○ at a barbecue   ○ at a fancy dinner

4. Which recipe uses the most ingredients?

   ○ Tom Kha Gai

   ○ Matzo Balls

   ○ Roasted Corn

5. Which recipe do you think you would like best?

   ○ Tom Kha Gai

   ○ Matzo Balls

   ○ Roasted Corn

6. The three children in this story have different cultural backgrounds. The recipes for their favorite foods originally came from three different countries. Which countries?

   ○ Thailand, China, Australia

   ○ Vietnam, Mexico, United States

   ○ Thailand, Russia, United States

What's Your Favorite?
Abbreviations

An **abbreviation** is a short way to write something. Recipes often include many different abbreviations. Match the abbreviations with the thing they represent.

tbsp.   • teaspoon

tsp.   • package

lb.   • ounce

qt.   • pound

oz.   • tablespoon

pkg.   • quart

You see some other abbreviations every day. Match these common abbreviations with their meaning.

a.m.   • miles per hour

m.p.h.   • Street

Dr.   • morning hours

Ave.   • Doctor

St.   • Avenue

Name_____

What's Your Favorite?
Reading a Recipe

Some words have special meanings when they are used in writing a recipe. Cut and paste to show what each direction means.

paste

paste

paste

paste

paste

paste

| Add the milk. | Butter the ear. | Spoon over rice. |
| Add a pinch of red pepper. | Sprinkle with salt. | Turn them every few minutes. |

Name_____

What's Your Favorite?
Find and Copy a Recipe

What is your favorite recipe?

Where did the recipe come from?

Copy it here.

_____
_____
_____
_____
_____
_____
_____

This recipe came from: _____

by _____

     Celebrating Diversity • EMC 795

In the Country

Mom hung up the telephone. She waved to Jenny. "Grandma just called. She's going to town. Would you like to ride along?"

"You bet!" Jenny answered. "Can we stop at the library? I'm done with my books."

Jenny was always ready to go to town. She liked to check out new library books. Within ten minutes she was in the front seat of her grandma's Ford. It moved down the road. She looked at the tall corn and green beans in the fields. The corn was taller than it had been a week ago. Soon farmers like her father would be cutting it.

After about fifteen minutes, Grandma pulled up to the library entrance. "I'm headed for the grocery store. I'll be back for you in one hour."

Jenny smiled and nodded. "Thanks, Gram. I'll be ready." Wow...an hour at the library! What a treat!

   Celebrating Diversity • EMC 795

In the City

"Sam, if you want to go to the library we need to leave now. The bus will be here in five minutes."

"I'm ready, Mom." Sam slung his backpack over his shoulder. He reached for the doorknob.

"Don't forget your pass," reminded Mom.

Sam and his mother hurried down the steps to the street. They walked to the corner and waited for the bus. The bus took them to the Muni station. They went into the station and through the turnstiles to the platform. After a few minutes the train pulled up. Some passengers got off. Sam and his mother got on. The train was crowded, so they stood side by side holding onto a pole.

The train moved quickly between stations. It paused only a few moments to let passengers get off or board. Sam and his mother stood quietly during the bustle. The conductor announced, "Next stop—Public Library." When the doors opened, Sam and his mother stepped off onto the platform. They went up the escalator. They came out just in front of the library.

Sam couldn't wait to get inside. "I'm headed for the mysteries, Mom. Come find me when you're ready."

In the Suburbs

"Hello, may I please speak to Mrs. Jones." Julie waited on the phone for her mom. "Mom, Vanessa said that she would take me to the library. Is that okay with you?...Great! We'll be home in an hour." Julie clicked the phone to turn it off. She turned to her baby-sitter. "Vanessa, Mom says it's fine to go to the library."

Julie grabbed four books. She ran out the front door of her house. She put the books in the basket on her bike and waited for Vanessa. Together the two girls rode their bikes down the streets to the library.

Julie lived in a small town. The houses stood side by side along the sidewalk. Julie and Vanessa waved to Peter when they passed his house. He was digging in his garden. Thomas and Fred were playing catch on the lawn at Fred's house. Maybelle was walking to the tennis courts.

The tall trees rustled their leaves. The breeze blew in cool bursts. At the library parking lot, Julie parked her bike in the bike rack. She grabbed her books and hurried inside. "Today's the day the new Eric Kimmel book is supposed to arrive. I can't wait to read it!"

Name_____

Questions about *Going to the Library*

1. What was the same about each of the stories?

_____

_____

_____

_____

2. What was different about the stories?

_____

_____

_____

_____

3. Describe a visit you would make to the library.

_____

_____

_____

_____

Name_____

Going to the Library
Vocabulary

Draw a line from the word to the picture that shows what it is.

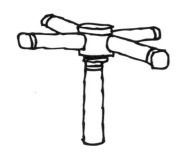

lawn

bike rack

turnstile

backpack

telephone

doorknob

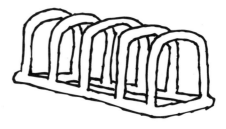

Name_____

Going to the Library
Classifying Words

Put each of the words from the stories into the right group.

Word Box					
bus	escalator	fields	corn	turnstile	farmers

In the Country	In a Big City
_____	_____
_____	_____
_____	_____
_____	_____
_____	_____

Think of some other words that would fit in each group.
Add them to the lists.

_____	_____
_____	_____
_____	_____

Name_____

Going to the Library
Where Do You Live?

Fill in a circle to answer each question.

1. Where do you live?

   ○ a big city   ○ a small city or town

   ○ the suburbs   ○ the country

2. How often do you go to the library?

   ○ once a week   ○ every day   ○ once a month

3. Which books do you like best?

   ○ mysteries   ○ nonfiction

   ○ animal stories   ○ _____

4. Who goes with you to the library?

   ○ Grandmother   ○ Mother

   ○ baby-sitter   ○ _____

Draw a picture to show the vehicle that takes you to the library.

He Changed America by Talking

Dr. Martin Luther King, Jr., was an important man. He was a father. He had a wife and four children. He was a minister and an author. Part of his job was giving a sermon every Sunday.

Dr. King talked to people every day. He spoke to many people in many places. He talked to people who were angry. He talked to people in jail. Presidents of the United States asked him to come and talk with them.

In 1963 Dr. King was thirty-four years old. He stood on the steps of the Lincoln Memorial in Washington, D.C. He talked to 250,000 people. The people listened as he talked. He talked about a dream that he had. He said, "I have a dream that my four little children will one day live in a nation where they will not be judged by the color of their skin but by the content of their character."

The people went home. They remembered Dr. King's speech. They remembered that he said all people were created equal. They remembered that he worked hard to make his dream come true.

Slowly the world began to change. People listened to Dr. King. They worked beside him. They fought bad laws with words and hard work.

Then in 1968 an angry man shot Dr. King. Dr. King died. People were afraid that Dr. King's dream would die with him. But people remembered his words. His talk changed America. His dream for his four children is coming true.

Name_____

Questions about *He Changed America by Talking*

1. Who was this story about?

   _____

2. What kind of a job did he have?

   _____

3. What did the story say that he did every day?

   _____

4. How did Dr. King and his followers fight bad laws?

   _____

5. What happened to Dr. King?

   _____

6. Do you think Dr. King's talk changed America?
   Tell why or why not.

   _____

   _____

   _____

Name_____

He Changed America by Talking
Understanding Big Words

Dr. Martin Luther King, Jr., believed in nonviolence.

- **Violent** means with great force.

- **Nonviolent** means without using force.

Write the word **violent** or **nonviolent** by each example below.

_____ Thomas punched Anthony because he laughed.

_____ Peter listened to Sergio give his opinion. Then Sergio listened to Peter.

_____ Suzi stepped on Maria's cookie because she was upset with Maria.

_____ Jenny wrote a letter asking for a bus stop closer to her house.

Dr. Martin Luther King, Jr., worked hard to stop injustice.

- **Just** means fair.   - **Unjust** means not fair.

Write **just** or **unjust** by each example below.

_____ Stefan had black hair, so he was the line leader.

_____ Van finished his work, so he had free time.

_____ Sophie's street was never fixed because the people who lived along the street didn't have much money.

_____ All library cardholders have to pay a fine when they are late in returning books to the library.

Name_____

He Changed America by Talking
Crossword Puzzle

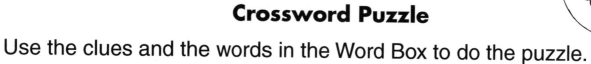

Use the clues and the words in the Word Box to do the puzzle.

Word Box	
father	children
leader	minister
author	talk
unjust	dream

Across

3. Dr. Martin Luther King, Jr., had four children. He was a _____.

4. Someone who leads is called a _____.

5. A _____ gives a sermon at church.

8. Dr. King dreamed that his _____ would not be judged by the color of their skin.

Down

1. Someone who writes books is an _____.

2. Dr. King's _____ lived on after he died.

6. One way to solve arguments is to _____.

7. Something that is unfair is _____.

Name_____

He Changed America by Talking
How Would You Like to Be Judged?

Dr. King said, "I have a dream that my four little children will one day live in a nation where they will not be judged by the color of their skin but by the content of their character."

Do the ideas below show that you are a good person?

Circle **yes** or **no**.

Your eyes are blue.	yes	no
Your hair is curly.	yes	no
You have money in your pocket.	yes	no
You work hard.	yes	no
You are honest.	yes	no
You respect others.	yes	no
You are skinny.	yes	no
You live in a big house.	yes	no

Write two ideas of your own.

Do they show that you are a good person?

Circle **yes** or **no**.

_____   yes   no

_____   yes   no

Kwanzaa
A New Holiday

A black teacher, Dr. Karenga, wanted a new holiday. He thought black families needed a time to think about the year that was ending. They needed a time to talk about what they thought was important.

Dr. Karenga went to Africa. He visited different countries. He wanted to learn about different African peoples. He wanted to bring good African values to America.

In 1966 Dr. Karenga used what he learned to start a new holiday. He called the holiday Kwanzaa. Today many families celebrate Dr. Karenga's holiday.

Kwanzaa is an African-American celebration. The holiday lasts seven days. Families make things together. They talk about the past year. They learn about important ideas. They light candles each night. Every night one more candle is lit. On the last night seven candles are lit. One candle is black. Three candles are green and three are red.

Celebrating Diversity • EMC 795

Kwanzaa
An African-American Celebration

7

There are seven letters in Kwanzaa.

There are seven days in the holiday.

There are seven symbols of Kwanzaa.

There are seven important principles.

There are seven candles in the Kwanzaa kinara.

Name_____

Questions about *Kwanzaa*

Circle **true** if the statement is true.
Circle **false** if the statement is false.

1. Kwanzaa has been celebrated for more than 100 years.

    true   false

2. Kwanzaa is an African-American festival.

    true   false

3. Kwanzaa is a celebration of the new year.

    true   false

4. Dr. Karenga based the principles of Kwanzaa on values he saw in Africa.

    true   false

5. The number six is important to Kwanzaa.

    true   false

6. Candles are a symbol of Kwanzaa.

    true   false

7. Kwanzaa is a family holiday.

    true   false

Name_____

Kwanzaa
Vocabulary

A **principle** is a truth or a rule. People who celebrate Kwanzaa learn about seven important principles. They think about ways they can use the principles in their lives.

Do you have important principles that you follow in your classroom?   yes   no

Do you have important principles that you follow at home?   yes   no

Write one principle that is important to you.

_____

Your **heritage** is a collection of values and traditions that have been passed down to you. People who celebrate Kwanzaa are celebrating their heritage.

Do you celebrate a holiday based on your heritage?   yes   no

Write one tradition that your family keeps.

_____

_____

_____

_____

Name_____

Kwanzaa
Thinking Creatively

Creativity is the principle of the sixth day of Kwanzaa. Be creative. Think of two new ways to carry your books home from school. Use your imagination. Draw pictures to show your ideas.

Celebrating Diversity • EMC 795

Kwanzaa
The Kinara

Read the information below. Then color the candles to show that you understand what you read.

The Kwanzaa candles stand in a candleholder called a kinara. There are three red candles on the left. There is one black candle in the center. There are three green candles on the right.

Only One
A Story About Ruby Bridges

"I want you to behave today. Don't be afraid. I'll be with you." That's what Ruby's mother told her.

Ruby was six years old, and she was going to a new school. People all over the world knew about Ruby and this special first day of school.

Ruby and her mother rode to school in a special car with four U.S. marshals. An angry crowd was standing outside the school. The people were shouting and throwing things.

Ruby walked behind the marshals into the school. All of the children in the school left when Ruby came. She and her mother sat in the principal's office. They watched the other boys and girls leave. They sat in the office the whole day.

The next day the marshals walked with Ruby to her classroom. There were many desks. There was one teacher. Ruby was the only student.

Each day Ruby went to school. Each day the teacher taught. No other students came. For one year Ruby was the only one.

Why was Ruby alone? It was 1960. A court had decided that children of all races should go to school together. Ruby was the first black child to go to a school with white children. Angry white parents kept their children at home.

Being the only one was hard. Some people were angry with Ruby's family. Her father lost his job. Her grandparents had to move. But Ruby's mother knew that all children should be able to go to a good school. Six-year-old Ruby helped to make that possible.

Look around your classroom. Are you the only one in some way? Are you the only one with black hair? Are you the only one with brown skin? Are you the only one with braces on your teeth? Are you the only one without a mom?

Don't be afraid. Remember Ruby Bridges. Remember the year she was the only one in her class. Be brave like Ruby. You can help make things better just like Ruby did.

Name_____

Questions about *Only One*

1. Who drove Ruby to school?

   ○ U.S. marshals   ○ her mother   ○ her father

2. What did Ruby see when she got to the school?

   ○ a nice playground   ○ an angry crowd   ○ the parking lot

3. Where did Ruby stay the first day of school?

   ○ on the playground   ○ in the classroom

   ○ in the principal's office

4. White families took their children home because

   ○ they thought it was a holiday

   ○ the marshals told them to

   ○ they didn't think a black child should go to their school

Think about a time when you were
the only one to do something.

_____

_____

_____

Draw your face to show how you felt.

Name_____

Only One
Learning New Words

To **segregate** means to separate people into groups because of their race.

Before Ruby went to school, many schools were **segregated**. Black girls and boys went to the black schools. White girls and boys went to the white schools. Ruby helped to **desegregate** the schools.

Write the correct word in each sentence.

segregated   **desegregated**

1. Before Ruby went to the new school, it was _____.

2. In 1960 the courts said that the schools should be

   _____.

3. A classroom of many races is _____.

4. A public restroom labeled "Whites Only" is a _____ restroom.

5. When a restaurant serves only people of one race it is a

   _____ restaurant.

6. Ruby was the "only one" for a year so other first-graders could

   be in a _____ classrom.

Name_____

Only One
How Would You Describe It?

Write a sentence describing each group. Circle the correct
word to tell whether the group is racially segregated or desegregated.

Digital Art

_____

_____

Is this a segregated group?   yes   no

Digital Art

_____

_____

Is this a segregated group?   yes   no

126

Name_____

Only One
How Did Ruby Feel?

Color this picture of Ruby Bridges. Then write about how you think Ruby must have felt when she was the only one.

_____

_____

_____

George Washington Carver
1864–1943

He could have added fortune to fame, but caring for neither, he found happiness and honor in being helpful to the world.

on his headstone at Tuskegee University

The little boy named George loved plants and he loved learning. By the time he was seven, people called him the Plant Doctor. He was a skinny child with a high voice. He sometimes stuttered when he talked. His slave mother had been stolen when he was a baby. He lived in the home of his master, George Carver.

When he was ten, George Washington Carver left home. He wanted to find a town with a school he could attend. He traveled through Missouri and Kansas. He went to schools that would accept black students. He worked as a cook. He opened a laundry to pay his own expenses.

In 1890 George began college. He studied art and agriculture. He was the first black graduate of Iowa State College. The famous inventor Thomas Edison asked George to work in his laboratory. George turned him down.

George wanted to help black people. He taught at Tuskegee Normal School, a college for black students in Alabama. He experimented with new ways to farm. He found new ways to use peanuts and other easy-to-grow crops. He was known as the Wizard of Tuskegee.

George Washington Carver worked and studied hard. He overcame hardships to become an important scientist. He never became rich. But his work helped people all over the world.

Name_____

Questions about *George Washington Carver*

1. Describe George Washington Carver as a young boy.

_____

_____

2. Why did George leave home when he was ten?

_____

3. What did George do when he graduated from college?

_____

_____

4. What made George famous?

○ He was very rich and he lived in a big house.

○ He traveled all over the world talking to workers.

○ He discovered many ways to use peanuts.

5. On his tombstone it says, "...he found happiness and honor in being helpful...." Tell what those words mean to you.

_____

_____

_____

Name_____

George Washington Carver
Vocabulary

Write the best word from the Word Box to complete each sentence.

Word Box		
stutter	inventor	expenses
agriculture	laundry	laboratory

1. George Washington Carver was responsible for his

   own _____.

2. Farmers study _____ to learn more about
   planting and raising crops.

3. Scientists sometimes do their experiments in

   a _____.

4. To _____ means to repeat the first sounds
   of words as you speak.

5. A place where clothes are washed and dried is called

   a _____.

6. An _____ makes or designs new things.

Name_____

George Washington Carver
Word Search

Find and circle the words below in the puzzle. Each word is something that George Washington Carver made from peanuts.

a	c	s	h	a	m	p	o	o	b	l
s	h	o	e	p	o	l	i	s	h	i
a	o	d	f	h	j	k	n	g	e	n
l	r	u	b	b	e	r	k	m	l	o
a	m	i	p	l	a	s	t	i	c	l
d	y	e	p	e	o	q	s	l	n	e
t	u	s	o	a	p	u	w	k	v	u
x	a	z	i	c	e	c	r	e	a	m
c	e	b	d	h	c	o	f	f	e	e
a	x	l	e	g	r	e	a	s	e	y

Word Box

axle grease	coffee	salad	shampoo	plastic	milk	dye
shoe polish	rubber	soap	ice cream	bleach	linoleum	ink

Name_____

George Washington Carver
How Do You Use Peanuts?

List five ways you use peanuts.

1._____

2._____

3._____

4._____

5._____

What is something new that you might use a peanut for?

_____

Would using a peanut in the new way help solve any problem?

Explain.   yes   no

_____

_____

_____

_____

_____

The Great Melting Pot

What is a "melting pot"? A cook can put different cheeses into one pot. When the cheeses melt, they blend together.

America is a great melting pot. Many people have come to America. People have special ways of doing things. They live together in America. Their many ways of life blend together.

Each time a new cheese is added to the cook's pot, the flavor changes. Each time new people come to America, America changes. Each person has a special "flavor." All the different flavors together make a unique blend.

 Celebrating Diversity • EMC 795

When a person goes to live in a new country, the person is called an immigrant. Many immigrants came to America before it was a country. Immigrants helped to build America.

Immigrants started America's government. They built cities, roads, and railways. They worked in fields, factories, and schools. Immigrants made music, wrote books, and painted memories. Immigrants were the "cheeses" that melted together in the pot.

The flavor of America is still changing. New immigrants bring new ideas. New immigrants bring new ways of doing things. Every American is part of the special American "taste."

Questions about *The Great Melting Pot*

Write **T** if the statement is true.

Write **F** if the statement is false.

_____ 1. America is a blend of all the different people who live in it.

_____ 2. An immigrant is a person who takes a short vacation.

_____ 3. Many immigrants came to America before it was a country.

_____ 4. The people who live in America are not all alike.

_____ 5. The differences in people "spoil the flavor."

_____ 6. Immigrants built America's cities and railways.

What does the word **immigrant** mean? Write a definition here.

_____

_____

_____

_____

_____

Name_____

The Great Melting Pot
Synonyms

Synonyms are words with almost the same meaning. Match the pairs of synonyms.

pot   • taste

blend   • cauldron

flavor   • mix

immigrant   • newcomer

Read each sentence. Complete each sentence using one of the words above.

1. The big black _____ was filled with soup.

2. Carlito is an _____ .

3. I stir the cocoa and whipped cream to _____ them.

4. The _____ of the soup changes when I add new things.

Name_____

The Great Melting Pot
My Way of Doing Things

Each American has his or her own way of doing some things. Draw a picture to show yourself doing each thing. Then share your paper with a friend. Do you do some things differently?

This is the way I celebrate my birthday.

This is what I eat for breakfast.

This is a game my family plays together.

Celebrating Diversity • EMC 795

The Great Melting Pot
Making Comparisons

Comparing America to a melting pot is one way of explaining America's diversity. Some people compare America to a salad bowl instead of a melting pot.

Salad Bowl	Melting Pot
Write some things you know about a salad bowl here.	Write some things you know about a melting pot here.

Think about America. Do you think America is more like a salad bowl or a melting pot? _____

Talk about the reasons why you think as you do.

Answer Key

Page 8
1. yes
2. no
3. Answers will vary.
   - 1 one   2 two   3 three
   - 4 four   5 five

Page 9
Students' drawings will vary.

two 2
four 4
one 1
three 3

Page 10
one
two
three
four
five
six
seven
eight
nine
ten

Page 14
1. c
2. d
3. Answers will vary, but may include:
   Two teams have special uniforms.
   Two teams are playing on special
   soccer fields.
   Two teams have special soccer
   shoes.
4. Answers will vary, but may include:
   All the players kick the ball.
   All the players look happy.
   All the players play on teams.
5. Answers will vary. One answer
   might be:
   I think both the teams like soccer.
   Even if you don't have a fancy
   uniform and shoes, you can enjoy
   the game.

Page 15
1. Slap, flap
2. card, hard
3. sun, fun
4. name, game

Page 16
Answers will vary.

Page 17
1. Game 1
2. Blue Team
3. 2 more goals
4. 13 goals

Page 20
1. Mexico
2. clay jars filled with treats
3. It is hit with a stick.
4. at both parties and picnics
5. a piece of candy
6. Answers will vary.

Page 21
Feet, meat, beet, wheat, cleat, and
parakeet should be marked with an **X**.
1. treat
2. neat
3. beat

Page 22
breakable—piggy bank, frame, vase,
toothpick house

unbreakable—bookend, book, ball,
mitt

Page 23
Drawings will vary.

Page 26

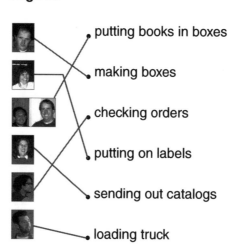

Page 27

warehouse | books | label

truck | boxes | catalog

Page 28
Responses will vary.

Page 29

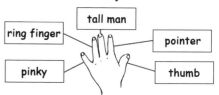

Answers will vary.

Page 32
1. 2
2. pick up something
3. eat their food
4. Answers will vary.

```
         tall man
ring finger        pointer
pinky              thumb
```

Page 33
sundae—spoon

hot dog—fingers

spaghetti—fork

meat and potatoes—fork

almond chicken and rice—chopsticks
or fork

pizza—fingers or fork

Page 34

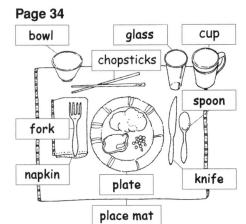

bowl, glass, cup, chopsticks, spoon, fork, napkin, plate, knife, place mat

Page 35
Answers will vary.

Page 39
1. a scrapbook

2. a story cloth

3. Answers will vary. One possible answer:
   Both the scrapbook and the story cloth have pictures that stand for important events. They help their owners remember things that have happened in the past.

4. Answers will vary. One possible answer:
   The scrapbook has photos and drawings pasted in it. The story cloth has pictures stitched on it.

5. Answers will vary.

Page 40
tractor—a vehicle used to pull equipment
memories—things that are remembered
stitched—sewed with thread
bamboo—a giant grass with hollow stems
journey—a long trip

1. memories
2. tractor
3. stitched
4. journey
5. bamboo

Page 41
Answers will vary.

Page 42
Answers will vary.

Page 45
1. a special kind of bread

2.

	Granny's Lefse	A Loaf of Bread
Main ingredient	potatoes	wheat
What does it look like?	a big pancake	a loaf
How do you eat it?	roll it up	by the slice

3. it has bumps on it

4. Answers will vary.

Page 46
lefse—flat rounds of potato bread
lutefisk—codfish soaked in lye

1. dough
2. rolls
3. coal
4. sausage
5. spatula
6. griddle

Page 47
1. Boil the potatoes.
2. Mash the potatoes.
3. Add butter, cream, salt, and flour.
4. Roll the dough.
5. Cook the bread.
6. Enjoy the yummy bread.

Page 48
Answers will vary. Some possible answers are:
   toast, sandwiches, croutons, breadsticks, buns, rolls

Page 51
1. He wanted to be a major-league pitcher.

2. He worked hard, practiced throwing and catching, and played baseball every chance he had.

3. Jim Abbott was born without a right hand.

4. If you set a goal and work hard, you can overcome challenges.

Page 52
pitch—to throw the ball for a batter to hit

starting pitcher—the player who is pitching at the beginning of a game

rookie—a first-year player

no-hitter—a game where no batter gets a hit

1. starting pitcher
2. no-hitter
3. rookie
4. pitch
5. rookie

Page 53
1. Jim decided to be a pitcher.

2. Jim joined a Little League team.

3. Jim pitched for his high school team.

4. Jim pitched for his college team.

5. Jim won an Olympic gold medal.

6. Jim pitched for the California Angels.

Page 54
Answers will vary.

Page 58
1. rice, corn, wheat
2. tip of the plant
3. golden brown
4. on the head
5. on the ear
6. the stalks, the leaves, and the ears

Page 59

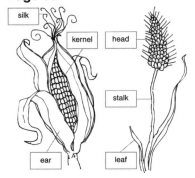

silk, kernel, head, stalk, ear, leaf

Page 60
Answers will vary.

Page 61
1. Farmers flood rice fields.

2. Farmers dig ditches between the rows of corn. They pump water into the ditches.

3. Farmers sometimes pump water and sometimes just let the rain irrigate the wheat.

4. Answers will vary.

Page 64
1. a race
2. in Alaska
3. all of the above
4. in a remote cabin
5. musher
6. Be independent and work hard.

Page 65

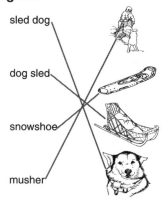

sled dog
dog sled
snowshoe
musher

Iditarod racers cross two mountain ranges.

The dogs ford ice-covered rivers.

The dogs must pull together in a team.

Susan Butcher chops her own firewood.

Page 66
fire, wood
grand, mother
some, one
near, by

fair, banks
It is near a river.

Answers will vary.

Page 67
Students' responses will vary. Correct responses for Susan Butcher are:

Place We Live
   location—Fairbanks, Alaska
   weather—cold and snowy

Things We Use
   television—no
   clock—no
   calendar—no

Things We Do
   walk dogs—yes
   visit with friends—no
   go to the store—no

Sentences will vary.

Page 69
1. runner
2. they wanted a better life
3. his track coach
4. hard work
5. running faster than anyone else has run
6. junior high track team, high school track team, U.S. Olympic team, college track team

Page 70
1. fast   4. fast   7. fast
2. slow   5. fast   8. slow
3. slow   6. slow   9. fast

Students' choices will vary.

Page 71
Answers will vary.

Page 72
dish, washer
cheer, leader
ship, builder
clock, maker

Page 75
1. Other students teased her because she looked different.

2. Evelyn's mother took her to ballet class.

3. Evelyn's school day was different. She went to school from 7:30 a.m. to 2:30 p.m. Then she went to ballet and practiced until dinner. She performed at a ballet theater after dinner.

4. She wants to tell them to work hard to make their dreams come true.

Page 76
A. 1. ballerina   3. company
   2. ballet   4. prima ballerina

B. Answers will vary.

Page 77
Apprentice—learner, beginner, needs to learn how

Master—teacher, a person with great skill, ready to share talent

Page 78
Answers will vary.

Page 81
1. "It's outta here!" means that the ball has been hit out of the playing area for a home run.

2. Babe Ruth, Roger Maris, Mark McGwire, Sammy Sosa

3. Answers will vary. They might include:
   They are both good hitters.
   They both play baseball.
   They both help other people.
   They are both fathers.

4. Answers will vary. They might include:
   Mark McGwire has light hair and light eyes.
   He went to college before he played baseball professionally.
   English was his first language.
   He was born in California.

   Sammy Sosa has dark hair and dark eyes.
   He signed a professional contract when he was 16.
   He has three children.
   He was born in the Dominican Republic.
   Spanish was his first language.

5. Answers will vary. One possible answer is:
   The two men are home run heroes with heart because they not only hit lots of home runs, but they also work hard to help other people.

Page 82
Circled sentences include:
Jeff hit a home run.
Swing the bat over the plate.
Try to hit the ball with the bat.
When you cross home plate you score a run.
The middle of the outfield is called center field.
The runner will circle the bases to score a run.

Page 83
Sammy Sosa gave computers to schools in the Dominican Republic.

His foundation supports children in the United States and the Dominican Republic.

Mark McGwire gives over $1 million to charity each year.

Answers will vary.

Page 84
1. 410 feet
2. 330 feet to 380 feet
3. 320 feet to 370 feet
4. yes

Page 87
1. He couldn't sit still. He had so much energy he was always moving. He was often in trouble.
2. Playing tennis was not a family activity. No one in Pancho's family had ever played tennis before.
3. Pancho watched other tennis players play and he practiced. He hit the ball hard and he moved fast.
4. Yes, Pancho's racket was important to him. It was so important that Pancho slept with it and talked to it.

Page 88
Court, *net*, and *racket* should be circled in each sentence.

1. tennis, not tennis
2. not tennis, tennis
3. not tennis, tennis

Page 89
Answers will vary.

Page 90
Answers will vary.

Page 92
1. Allen Say decided he wanted to draw cartoons when he was six years old.
2. He lived alone and he was only twelve years old.
3. Allen came to America when he was sixteen.
4. He is a bridge between two different countries.
5. Answers will vary.

Page 93
cartoonist—someone who uses pictures to tell a story

apprentice—a student learning a skill from a master

apartment—a rented room or rooms

storyteller—someone who uses words to tell a story

Answers will vary.

Page 94
Pictures will vary.

Page 95
Students should draw a red circle around Japan and a blue circle around California.

Pacific Ocean

Page 99
1. for supper
2. when you're sick
3. at a barbecue
4. Tom Kha Gai
5. Answers will vary.
6. Thailand, Russia, United States

Page 100
tbsp.—tablespoon
tsp.—teaspoon
lb.—pound
qt.—quart
oz.—ounce
pkg.—package

a.m.—morning hours
m.p.h.—miles per hour
Dr.—Doctor
Ave.—Avenue
St.—Street

Page 101

Page 102
Recipes will vary.

Page 106
1. The boy or girl in each story was going to the library.
2. The children lived in different places, and they used different kinds of transportation to get to the libraries.
3. Answers will vary.

Page 107

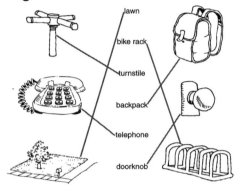

Page 108
In the Country—fields, corn, farmers

In a Big City—bus, escalator, turnstile

Additional words will vary.

Page 109
Answers will vary.

Page 112
1. Dr. Martin Luther King, Jr.
2. He was a minister and an author.
3. He talked to people.
4. They fought with words and hard work.
5. He was shot by an angry man.
6. Answers will vary.

Page 113
violent
nonviolent
violent
nonviolent

unjust
just
unjust
just

Page 114

Page 115
no, no, no, yes, yes, yes, no, no

New ideas will vary.

Page 118
1. false
2. true
3. false
4. true
5. false
6. true
7. true

Page 119
Answers will vary.

Page 120
Answers will vary.

Page 121
Candles should be colored so that the three on the left are red, the one in the center is black, and the three on the right are green.

Page 124
1. U.S. marshals

2. an angry crowd

3. in the principal's office

4. they didn't think a black child should go to their school

Drawings will vary.

Page 125
1. segregated
2. desegregated
3. desegregated
4. segregated
5. segregated
6. desegregated

Page 126
Sentences will vary.

yes

no

Page 127
Responses will vary.

Page 130
1. Descriptions will vary. One possible response: George Washington Carver was a skinny little black boy with a high voice, but he knew a lot about plants. People even called him the Plant Doctor.

2. He wanted to find a school that would accept him as a student.

3. He taught at Tuskegee Normal School and experimented with different methods of farming.

4. He discovered many ways to use peanuts.

5. Answers will vary.

Page 131
1. expenses
2. agriculture
3. laboratory
4. stutter
5. laundry
6. inventor

Page 132

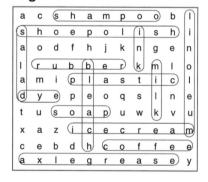

Page 133
Answers will vary. Some possible uses for peanuts include: peanut butter, roasted peanuts, peanut sauce, monkey food, topping for sundaes, chopped and stuck onto a caramel apple.

Page 136
1. T
2. F
3. T
4. T
5. F
6. T

Definitions will vary. One definition might be:

An immigrant is a person who goes to live in a new country.

Page 137
pot—cauldron
blend—mix
flavor—taste
immigrant—newcomer

1. pot or cauldron

2. immigrant or newcomer

3. blend or mix

4. flavor or taste

Page 138
Answers will vary.

Page 139
Answers will vary. Some possible responses follow:

Salad Bowl
many ingredients
ingredients usually chopped
ingredients are identifiable
you can pick out individual
   ingredients

Melting Pot
Ingredients blend together and lose
   individual identity.
You can't pick out individual
   ingredients.

Answers will vary.